crochet
COWLS

crochet
COWLS

Sharon Hernes Silverman

**STACKPOLE
BOOKS**

Lanham   Boulder   New York   London

Published by Stackpole Books
An imprint of Globe Pequot
Distributed by NATIONAL BOOK NETWORK
800-462-6420

Cover design by Tessa J. Sweigert
Crochet charts by Lindsey Stephens
Photographs by Daniel Shanken (model photography), Alan Wycheck,
and Sharon Hernes Silverman
Standard yarn weight system chart and skill level symbols used
courtesy of the Craft Yarn Council of America (CYCA),
www.yarnstandards.com.

British Library Cataloguing-in-Publication Information available.

Library of Congress Cataloging-in-Publication Data is available.
ISBN 978-0-8117-1674-1 (paperback)
ISBN 978-0-8117-6536-7 (e-book)

♾™ The paper used in this publication meets the minimum require-
ments of American National Standard for Information Science—
Permanence of Paper for Printed Library Materials, ANSI/NISO
Z39.48-1992.

Contents

Introduction

Welcome to *Crochet Cowls*, your source for knockout neckwear patterns! The fifteen original designs span a variety of styles and crochet techniques. Whether you're looking for an elegant accessory, a casual cowl to pair with jeans, or something to keep you toasty in the dead of winter, you'll find inspiration in these pages.

This book is for people who are already comfortable with basic crochet stitches (chain, single crochet, double crochet). Before you start the projects, review the basic instructions in the back of the book if needed.

Several of the projects are done in Tunisian crochet. This technique creates fabrics that look knitted or woven. All of the basics are explained in the back of the book. If you are new to Tunisian crochet and want more detailed instructions on getting started with the technique, you might find *Tunisian Crochet: The Look of Knitting with the Ease of Crocheting* helpful.

Instructions for special stitches or techniques are included with the pattern or are covered in the Techniques section. Step-by-step photographs appear throughout. In addition, symbol charts are provided. These focus on specific parts of the patterns that benefit from visual representation, and are included to help make the patterns easy to understand. See the Techniques section for instructions on how to read charts.

Reference material, including a list of abbreviations, supplier information for yarn and hooks, and crochet associations, appears at the end of the book. There is also a Visual Index in which you can see all of the projects at a glance.

Happy crocheting!

Projects

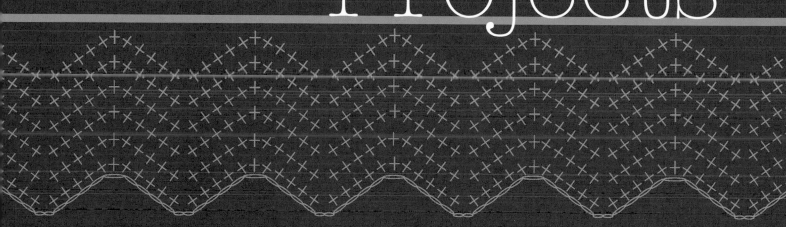

Art Deco
Skyline

ows of silvery beads against a black background
R *evoke the beautiful Art Deco buildings that grace the*
Manhattan skyline. This isn't a quick project or one that's
easily portable, but it's well worth the time and effort.

SKILL LEVEL

INTERMEDIATE +

MEASUREMENTS

4 in. (10.2 cm) wide by 38.5 in. (98 cm) in
    circumference

MATERIALS

Lace

Aunt Lydia's Crochet Thread Classic 10 distributed by
    Red Heart (100% mercerized cotton; 8 oz./225 g,
    1,000 yd./914 m)

  » Black, 1 ball

1,080 size six silvertone beads (plus about 50 extra in
    case any are defective)
Big-eye beading needle
U.S. size G-6 (4.25 mm) crochet hook
Tapestry needle

GAUGE

16 stitches and 16 rows in hdc = 4 in. (10.2 cm),
    blocked
For gauge swatch, ch 31. Last 2 chs count as first hdc
    on Row 1.
Row 1: Hdc into third ch from hook and in each ch
    across. Total 30 hdc.
Row 2: Ch 2 (counts as hdc), turn. Sk st at base of chs.
    Hdc in each st across, ending with final hdc in top
    of turning ch. Total 30 hdc.
Repeat Row 2 until swatch measures at least 4.5 in.
    (11.4 cm).

Stringing Beads

To string beads, use a big-eye beading needle.

Be careful: Both ends are quite sharp. Rather than holding the beads and trying to manipulate the needle into the hole, pour some beads onto a table or into a shallow dish and pick them up with the end of the needle. When you are done with the needle, return it to its original packaging so nobody gets poked.

1. Put the yarn through the large eye of the beading needle.

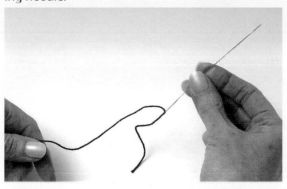

2. Use the end of the needle to pick up several beads.

3. Slide the beads past the needle onto the yarn.

4. Push the beads down the yarn away from the needle, spreading them out as you go.

5. Remove yarn from needle.

Special Stitches

Beaded Half Double Crochet (bhdc)

Yarn over, insert hook in next st, yo, pull up lp (3 lps on hook). Slide the next bead into position up close to the hook. (You can hold it in place with the thumb and third finger of your non-hook hand.) Yo, pull through all 3 lps. Bead will show on other side of work.

Beaded Chain (bch)

Slide the next bead into position up close to the hook. (You can hold it in place with the thumb and finger of your non-hook hand.) Yo, pull through lp.

Pattern Notes

» Beads are prestrung and pulled into place as the pattern specifies. The remainder of the prestrung beads have to be moved out of the way as you go along. How many beads to string is a matter of personal preference. Some crocheters string all the beads before starting to crochet; others string just one or two rows of beads at first. In this project there are 180 beads on every other row.

  If you string less than the full amount of beads, you will have to stop when you run out. Cut the yarn, prestring beads onto the next segment of yarn, rejoin the yarn, and resume crocheting. Ideally, do this at the end of a row. (Alternatively, if you don't have much yarn left, you can unroll the ball and string the beads from the other end.)

  Be careful to slide the beads gently so they do not damage the yarn. Move just a few at a time, starting with the ones that are farthest from your hook. If you find a bead that is catching on the yarn, gently use a pliers (and eye protection) to break it and remove it.

» Beads are slid into place and crocheted on wrong side rows, but they will show on the right side. There are 30 unbeaded stitches between each group of 20 beaded stitches.

» Cowl is worked flat, then seamed into a loop.

Pattern

Prestring beads.

Ch 301. Last 2 chs count as first hdc on Row 1.

Row 1 (RS): Hdc in third ch from hook and in each ch across. Total 300 hdc.

Row 2: Ch 2 (counts as hdc here and throughout), turn. Sk st at base of chs, hdc in each of next 29 sts, bhdc in each of next 20 sts. *Hdc in each of next 30 sts, bhdc in each of next 20 sts. Repeat from * to end.

Row 3: Ch 2, turn. Sk st at base of chs. Hdc in next st and in each st across.

Row 4: Ch 1, bch (counts as bhdc), turn. Sk st at base of chs. Work 4 bhdc. *Hdc in each of next 30 sts, bhdc in each of next 20 sts. Repeat from * until 15 sts remain. Bhdc in each of next 15 sts.

Row 5: Repeat Row 3.

Row 6: Ch 1, bch (counts as bhdc), turn. Sk st at base of chs. Work 9 bhdc. *Hdc in each of next 30 sts, bhdc in each of next 20 sts. Repeat from * until 10 sts remain. Bhdc in each of next 10 sts.

Row 7: Repeat Row 3.

Row 8: Ch 1, bch (counts as bhdc), turn. Sk st at base of chs. Work 14 bhdc. *Hdc in each of next 30 sts, bhdc in each of next 20 sts. Repeat from * until 5 sts remain. Bhdc in each of next 5 sts.

Row 9: Repeat Row 3.

Row 10: Ch 1, bch (counts as bhdc), turn. Sk st at base of chs. Work 19 bhdc. *Hdc in each of next 30 sts, bhdc in each of next 20 sts. Repeat from * until 30 sts remain. Hdc in each of next 30 sts.

Row 11: Repeat Row 3.

Row 12: Repeat Row 8.

Row 13: Repeat Row 3.

Row 14: Repeat Row 6.

Row 15: Repeat Row 3.

Row 16: Repeat Row 4.

Row 17: Repeat Row 3.

Row 18: Repeat Row 2.

Row 19: Repeat Row 3. Fasten off.

FINISHING AND ASSEMBLY

Weave in ends. With WS facing you, seam short ends together, making sure the beaded rows line up.

Art Deco Skyline
Section of Pattern

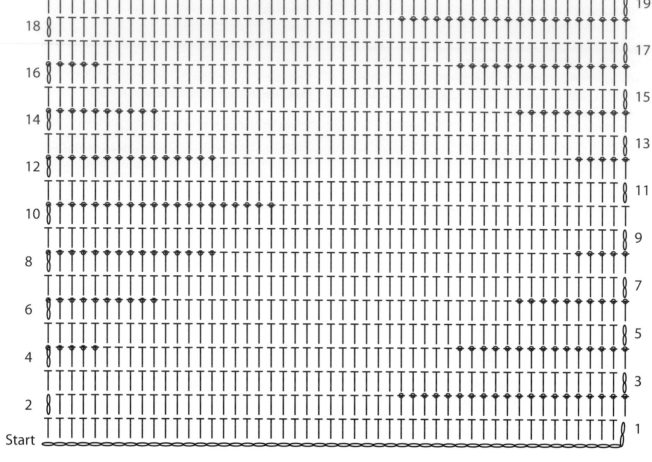

○ = chain stitch   ⊤ = beaded half double crochet
⊤ = half double crochet

⊙ = beaded chain stitch

Atlantic Ice

A luxurious silk-mohair blend yarn provides lots of warmth yet very little weight. This stylish neck warmer is worked with two strands held together to change the color from subtle to vivid and back again.

SKILL LEVEL

EXPERIENCED

MEASUREMENTS

12.5 in. (31.75 cm) by 24 in. (61 cm) in
  circumference

MATERIALS

Lace

Rowan Kidsilk Haze (70% mohair, 30% silk;
  0.88 oz./25 g, 229 yd./210 m)

> » Color A: Ghost (642), 2 balls
> » Color B: Atlantic (609), 1 ball

U.S. size G-6 (4.25 mm) crochet hook
Tapestry needle

GAUGE

15 stitches and 9 rows in dc = 4 in. (10.2 cm),
  blocked
For gauge swatch, ch 28. Last 3 chs count as first dc
  on Row 1.
Row 1: Dc into fourth ch from hook and in each ch
  across. Total 26 dc.
Row 2: Ch 3 (counts as dc), turn. Sk st at base of
  chs. Dc in each st across, ending with final dc in
  top of turning ch. Total 26 dc.
Repeat Row 2 until swatch measures at least 4.5 in.
  (11.4 cm).

Pattern Notes

» Mohair requires a gentle touch. Do not pull your stitches tight. Make sure that the balls of yarn are not pulling on your stitches, and that both strands have the same tension.

If you have not worked with mohair before, I recommend two things: 1) Make the mohair swatch as specified above. Doing double crochet stitches with two strands held together is a simple way to get comfortable with such fine, fuzzy yarn. 2) For practice, crochet Rows 1–7 of the pattern using one strand of worsted weight yarn and a corresponding size hook. That way, you'll be familiar with the pattern when you start using the mohair. Keep your worsted swatch handy—along with the written pattern and symbol chart—as a visual reminder of what the pattern should look like as you make your mohair project.

» The commas are very important in this pattern. Read the pattern thoroughly before you start to crochet, and refer to the symbol chart to make sure you understand stitch placement and which stitches are skipped.

Pattern

Using two strands of A held together, ch 94.

Row 1: [Dc, ch 3, dc] in fourth ch from hook. *Ch 3, sk 3 ch, sc in each of next 3 ch, ch 3, sk 3 ch, [dc, ch 3, dc] in next ch. Repeat from * to end.

Row 2: Ch 3, turn. Sk first dc. *7 dc into ch-3 sp, ch 3, sk [1 dc, 3 ch, 1 sc], sc in next sc, ch 3, sk [1 sc, 3 ch, 1 dc]. Repeat from *, ending with 7 dc in last ch-3 sp.

Row 3: Ch 1, turn. Sk first dc. Sc in each of next 6 dc. *Ch 5, sk [3 ch, 1 sc, 3 ch], sc in each of next 7 dc. Repeat from * to end.

Row 4: Ch 6, turn. Sk first 2 sc. Sc in each of next 3 sc (the center 3 sc of 7). *Ch 3, sk [2 sc, 2 ch], [dc, ch

3, dc] in next ch, ch 3, sk [2 ch, 2 sc], sc in each of next 3 sc. Repeat from *, ending with ch 3, sk 1 sc, dc in ch-1.

Row 5: Ch 6, turn. Sk [first dc, 3 ch, 1 sc]. *Sc in next sc, ch 3, sk [1 sc, 3 ch, 1 dc], 7 dc in next ch-3 sp, ch 3, sk [1 dc, 3 ch, 1 sc]. Repeat from *, ending with ch 3, dc in third ch of ch-6.

Row 6: Ch 5, turn. Sk [first dc, 3 ch, 1 sc, 3 ch]. *Sc in each of next 7 dc, ch 5, sk [3 ch, 1 sc, 3 ch]. Repeat from *, ending with ch 5, sc in third ch of ch-6.

Row 7: Ch 3, turn. Sk [first sc, 2 ch]. *[Dc, ch 3, dc] in next ch, ch 3, sk [2 ch, 2 sc], sc in each of next 3 sc, ch 3, sk [2 sc, 2 ch]. Repeat from *, ending with [dc, ch 3, dc] in third ch of ch-5, changing one strand of A to B when 2 lps remain on hook in final st. Cut the dropped strand of A, leaving a 4-inch (10.2 cm) tail.

Rows 8–13: Repeat Rows 2–7 using one strand A and one strand B. Change A to B when 2 lps remain on hook in final st at end of Row 13. Cut the dropped strand of A, leaving a 4-inch (10.2 cm) tail.

Rows 14–19: Repeat Rows 2–7 using two strands B. Change one strand of B to A when 2 lps remain on hook in final st at end of Row 19. Cut the dropped strand of B, leaving a 4-inch (10.2 cm) tail.

Rows 20–25: Repeat Rows 2–7 using one strand A and one strand B. Change B to A when 2 lps remain on hook in final st at end of Row 25. Cut the dropped strand of B, leaving a 4-inch (10.2 cm) tail.

Rows 26–31: Repeat Rows 2–7 using two strands A. Fasten off both strands.

FINISHING

Lightly steam block on WS if desired.

With WS facing you, use the tails from the color changes to seam the cowl closed. Weave in any remaining ends.

Atlantic Ice
Section of Pattern

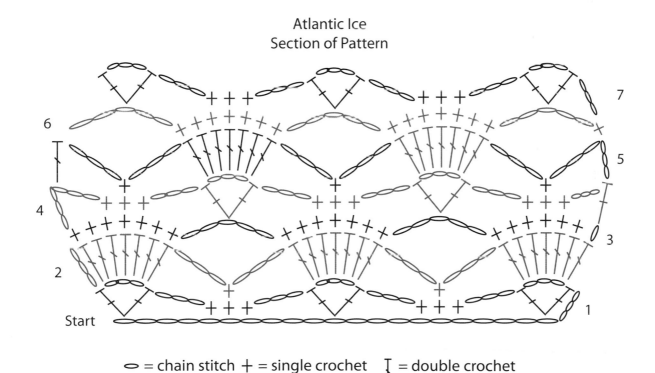

∘ = chain stitch + = single crochet ⊤ = double crochet

Boxy
Loxy

*R*elief stitches create three-dimensional frames around the rectangles in this cowl. It takes a little practice to manage stitches as long as quintuple trebles, but take your time and you'll be able to handle all of those loops with no problem. A chunky square button echoes the geometric theme.

SKILL LEVEL

EXPERIENCED

MEASUREMENTS

9 in. (23 cm) by 34 in. (86.25 cm) around shoulders

MATERIALS

Medium

Brown Sheep Co., Inc., Lamb's Pride Superwash worsted (100% wool; 3.5 oz./100 g, 200 yd./183 m)

> » Color A: Onyx (SW05), 1 skein
> » Color B: Sunshine Yellow (SW169), 1 skein
> » Color C: Blaze (SW145), 1 skein
> » Color D: White Frost (SW11), 1 skein
> » Color E: Bon Vivant Blue (SW176), 1 skein

U. S. size I-9 (5.5 mm) crochet hook
Tapestry needle
Yellow button, 1.5 in. (3.75 cm) square
Matching sewing thread
Sewing needle

GAUGE

12 stitches and 16 rows in sc = 4 in. (10.2 cm), blocked
For gauge swatch, ch 21. Sc in second ch from hook and in each ch across. Total 20 sc. Turn.
Row 1: Ch 1. Sc in each sc across. Turn.
Repeat Row 1 until swatch measures at least 4.5 in. (11.4 cm).

Special Stitches

Double Treble/Raised Front (dtr/rf)

This stitch is worked around the post 5 rows below the current row. In the pattern, you will be able to tell where to place the stitch because the color will match up. *Note: The photos show a project that used two strands held together. The cowl only uses one strand at a time.*

1. Wrap yo 3 times for double treble.

2. Locate the target stitch 5 rows below. You will work around the post of this stitch, keeping the hook to the front of the work.

3. Insert hook around post, yo, pull up lp. [Yo, pull through 2 lps] 4 times. Dtr/rf completed.

The photo shows a pair of dtr/rf.

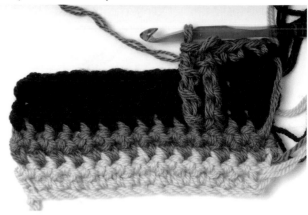

Quintuple Treble/Raised Front (quintr/rf)

This stitch is worked around the post 9 rows below the current row. In the pattern, you will be able to tell where to place the stitch because the color will match up.

1. Wrap yo 6 times for quintuple treble.

2. Locate the target stitch 9 rows below. You will work around the post of this stitch, keeping the hook to the front of the work. Use your index finger to help the loops stay in place around the hook.

3. Insert hook around post, yo, pull up lp. [Yo, pull through 2 lps] 7 times. Quintr/rf completed. The photo shows a pair of completed quintr/rf.

Pattern

With A, ch 93. *Note: To make the garment wider around the shoulders, add stitches in multiples of 10.*

Row 1 (RS): Sc into second ch from hook and in each ch to end. Total 92 sc.

Row 2: Ch 1, turn. Sc in each sc across. Change to B when 2 lps remain on hook in last st. Turn.

NOTE: *To change colors, drop first color when 2 lps remain on final st of row. Begin working with new color. Cut old color, leaving about a 4-inch (10.2 cm) tail.*

Rows 3–4: Repeat Row 2, changing to C when 2 lps remain at end of Row 4.

Rows 5–8: Repeat Row 2, changing to B when 2 lps remain at end of Row 8.

Row 9: With B, ch 1, turn. Sc into each of the first 3 sts, *[dtr/rf around next st 5 rows below (also color B)] twice, sc into each of next 4 sts, [dtr/rf around next st 5 rows below] twice, sc into each of next 2 sts. Repeat from * across, ending with sc into last st.

Row 10: Ch 1, turn. Sc into each st across, changing to A when 2 lps remain at end of row.

Row 11: With A, ch 1, turn. Sc into first st, *[quintr/rf around next st 9 rows below (also color A)] twice, sc into each of next 8 sts. Repeat from * to last st, sc in that st.

Row 12: Ch 1, turn. Sc into each st across.

Rows 13–14: Repeat Row 2 twice, changing to D when 2 lps remain at end of Row 14.

Rows 15–16: Repeat Rows 3–4, changing to E when 2 lps remain at end of Row 16.

Rows 17–20: Repeat Rows 5–8, changing to D when 2 lps remain at end of Row 20.

Rows 21–22: Repeat Rows 9–10, changing to A when 2 lps remain at end of Row 22.

Rows 23–24: Repeat Rows 11–12.

Rows 25–26: Repeat Row 2 twice, changing to E when 2 lps remain at end of Row 26.

Rows 27–28: Repeat Rows 3–4, changing to B when 2 lps remain at end of Row 28.

Rows 29–32: Repeat Rows 5–8, changing to E when 2 lps remain at end of Row 32.

Rows 33–34: Repeat Rows 9–10, changing to A when 2 lps remain at end of Row 34.

Rows 35–36: Repeat Rows 11–12. Fasten off.

FINISHING

Weave in ends. Lightly steam block on WS.

Short Edge (Button Side)

Row 1: With RS facing you, join A at top corner of short side. Ch 1, sc evenly down row ends along short side.

Row 2: Ch 1, turn. Sc in each st.

Rows 3–4: Repeat Row 2. Fasten off. Weave in ends.

Short Edge (Button Loop Side)

Row 1: With RS facing you, join A at bottom corner of short side. Ch 1, sc evenly along row ends.

Row 2: Ch 1, turn. Sc in each st.

Row 3 (button loop row): Ch 1, turn. Sc in each st until 7 sts remain. Ch 11, sk 2 sts, sc in remaining sts. *Note: If the size or shape of your button is different from the one in the sample, adjust the length of your chain accordingly. The button loop should fit over the button smoothly and not be loose when the cowl is buttoned.*

Row 4: Ch 1, turn. Sc in each of first 5 sts. Work 11 sc around ch loop. Sc in each remaining st. Fasten off. Weave in ends. Lightly steam block on WS if desired.

Sew button onto yellow square opposite button loop with sewing needle and matching thread.

Boxy Loxy
Section of Pattern

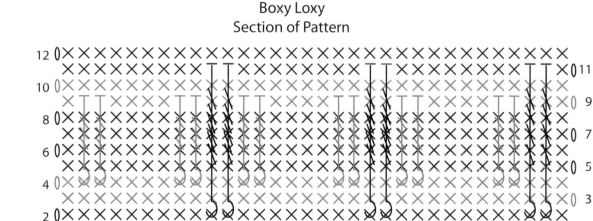

○ = chain stitch ✕ = single crochet

⟊ = double treble/raised front ⟊ = quintuple treble/raised front

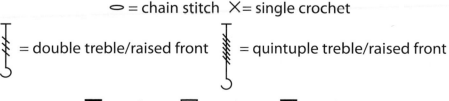

■ = Color A ■ = Color B ■ = Color C

Chepstow Cowl

*W*oven stitch—a simple combination of single crochet and chain stitches—gives a unique texture to this warm, versatile neck warmer. A large hook and two strands of yarn held together make this a quick and easy project.

SKILL LEVEL

EASY

MEASUREMENTS
10 in. (25.5 cm) by 28 in. (71 cm) in circumference

MATERIALS

Medium

Red Heart Boutique Unforgettable (100% acrylic; 3.5 oz./100 g, 280 yd./256 m)

   » Cappuccino (9942), 2 skeins

U.S. size M/13 (9 mm) crochet hook
2 stitch markers
Tapestry needle

GAUGE
With two strands of yarn held together, 13 stitches and 13 rows in pattern = 4 in. (10.2 cm), blocked. *Note: Count each ch and each sc individually, not pairs of stitches.*
For gauge swatch, ch 20 with two strands held together. Follow pattern.

Pattern

Note: Project is worked with two strands held together.
With two strands of yarn held together, ch 90.
Row 1 (RS): Sc in second ch from hook. *Ch 1, sk 1
ch, sc in next ch. Repeat from * across.
Row 2: Ch 1, turn. *Sc in ch sp, ch 1, sk 1 sc. Repeat
from * across, ending with sc in turning ch.

*Placement of the single crochet stitches in the chain
spaces. Note: The photo shows only one strand of
yarn; you'll be working with two strands.*

NOTE: *You should have 45 sc on each row. To help you
find the turning chain in which to work the final stitch on
a row, you can place a stitch marker in the turning chain
when you make it.*

Rows 3–30: Repeat Row 2. Fasten off.

FINISHING
Lightly steam block on WS. Weave in ends.
With WS facing you, use one strand of yarn to seam
the short sides together.

Chepstow Cowl
Section of Pattern

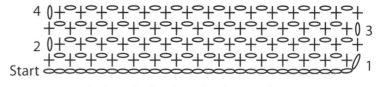

○ = chain stitch   + = single crochet

Chunky
Lime Cowl

*T*he stitches are big and chunky but the yarn is smooth and creamy in this deliciously warm Tunisian crochet cowl.

SKILL LEVEL

EASY

MEASUREMENTS
15 in. (38 cm) by 37 in. (94 cm) in circumference

MATERIALS

**Super
Bulky**

Bernat Baby Blanket (100% polyester; 10.5 oz./
   300 g, 258 yd./234 m)

>> Lemon Lime (04223), 1 ball

U.S. size Q-16 (15.75 mm) Tunisian crochet hook
Tapestry needle with big enough eye to thread
   yarn through, or U.S. size K-10½ (6.5 mm) hook
   to weave in ends
Matching sewing thread
Sewing needle

GAUGE
7 stitches and 8 rows in Tks = 4 in. (10.2 cm),
   blocked

Special Stitches

Tunisian Purl Stitch Into Foundation Chain

1. Bring the yarn to the front of the work.

2. Insert the hook into the second chain from the hook.

3. Let the yarn go. Bring it toward you in front of the stitch, then back under the hook.

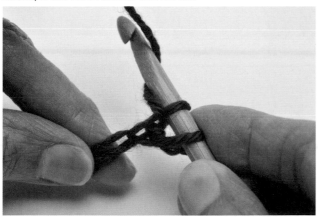

4. Yarn over, pull up a loop with that yarn. There will be two loops on the hook.

5. Continue in this fashion all the way across, adding a loop to the hook with each stitch. Notice the "purl bump" in the front of each stitch. Count the loops—you should have the same number as the foundation chain.

6. Do not turn. Work standard return (yo, pull through 1 lp, *yo, pull through 2 lps, repeat from * until 1 lp remains on hook).

Tunisian Knit Stitch Into Foundation Chain

1. Insert hook where indicated.

2. Yarn over, pull up loop. This adds 1 stitch to the hook and completes the stitch.

Pattern Notes

» For additional step-by-step instructions on how to work Tunisian knit and purl stitches, see pages 97–100.

Pattern

Ch 61.

Row 1: Tps in second ch from hook, Tps in next ch. *Tks in each of next 2 chs, Tps in each of next 2 chs. Repeat from * until 2 sts remain. Tks in each of next 2 sts. Return.

Row 2: Sk first vertical bar. Tps in each of next 2 sts. *Tks in each of next 2 sts, Tps in each of next 2 sts. Repeat from * until 2 sts remain. Tks in each of next 2 sts. Return.

Row 3: Repeat Row 2.

Row 4: Sk first vertical bar. Tks in each st across. Return.

Rows 5–21: Repeat Row 4.

Row 22: Sk first vertical bar. Tps in each of next 2 sts. *Tks in each of next 2 sts, Tps in each of next 2 sts. Repeat from * until 2 sts remain. Tks in each of next 2 sts. Return.

Row 23: Repeat Row 22.

Row 24: Sk first vertical bar. Sc in each st across, entering the stitch as for Tps or Tks to remain in pattern. (You will not be adding loops to the hook.) Fasten off.

FINISHING

Weave in ends. Gently steam block on WS if desired.

With WS facing you, use a sewing needle and a double thickness of sewing thread to seam short sides together.

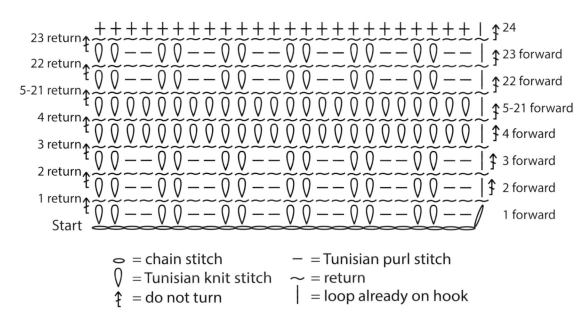

Chunky Lime Cowl
Section of Pattern

○ = chain stitch − = Tunisian purl stitch

◊ = Tunisian knit stitch ~ = return

↕ = do not turn | = loop already on hook

+ = single crochet, entering stitch as Tps or Tks to remain in pattern

Double-Strand Delight

*A*utumn colors and plenty of textured stitches make this project fun to stitch and lovely to wear. It's the perfect finish for a jean jacket as the weather turns cool.

SKILL LEVEL

INTERMEDIATE

MEASUREMENTS

4 in. (10 cm) by 48 in. (122 cm) in circumference

MATERIALS

Super Fine

Filatura Cervinia Perlina distributed by Plymouth Yarn Company, Inc. (100% extra fine merino wool; 1.75 oz./50 g, 250 yd./230 m)

> » Color A: Pumpkin (12), 2 balls
> » Color B: Mustard (9), 1 ball
> » Color C: Navy (5), 1 ball

U.S. size G-6 (4.25 mm) crochet hook
Tapestry needle

GAUGE

With two strands held together, 18 stitches and 11 rows in dc = 4 in. (10.2 cm), blocked

For gauge swatch, with two strands held together ch 32. Last 3 chs count as first dc on Row 1.

Row 1: Dc into fourth ch from hook and in each ch across. Total 30 dc.

Row 2: Ch 3 (counts as dc), turn. Sk st at base of chs. Dc in each st across, ending with final dc in top of turning ch. Total 30 dc.

Repeat Row 2 until swatch measures at least 4.5 in. (11.4 cm)

Special Stitch

Large Cluster (LC)

The large cluster joins 5 dc stitches together. This is achieved by working each stitch up to the step before completion, then closing all 5 at once. The stitch is finished by pulling through the remaining 2 lps.

1. [Yo, insert hook as instructed, yo, pull up lp, yo pull through 2 lps] in same spot 5 times. Total 6 lps on hook. *Note: The photos show the stitch worked with only one strand of yarn; you will hold two strands together as you work this pattern.*

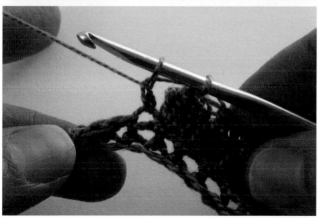

2. Yo, pull through 5 lps.

3. Yo, pull through remaining 2 lps.

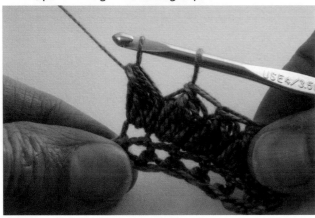

4. Large cluster completed.

Color Sequence

Note: The pattern is worked with two strands held together. When instructed to drop one color and replace it with another, cut the first yarn, leaving about a 4-inch (10.2 cm) tail.

The color sequence is as follows:

Row 1: A and B
Row 2: A and C
Row 3: B and C
Row 4: A and B
Rows 5–7: Two strands A
Row 8: A and B
Row 9: B and C
Row 10: A and C
Row 11: A and B

Pattern

Using one strand of A and one strand of B held together, ch 177.

Row 1 (RS): Sc into second ch from hook and in each ch across. Total 176 sc. Drop B, pick up C when 2 lps remain in final st at end of row.

Row 2: Ch 3, turn. Sk first sc. *LC in next sc, ch 1, sk 1 sc. Repeat from * across, ending with LC. Total 88 LC. Drop A, pick up B when 2 lps remain in final st at end of row.

Row 3: Ch 3, turn. Sk first LC. *LC in ch sp, ch 1, sk LC. Repeat from * across, working final LC in ch-3 sp. Drop C, pick up A when 2 lps remain in final st at end of row.

Row 4: Repeat Row 3. Drop B and pick up second strand of A when 2 lps remain in final st at end of row.

Row 5: Ch 3, turn. Dc in the top of each cluster and in each ch sp across.

Row 6: Ch 3, turn. Sk st at base of chs. Dc in each st across, ending with a dc in top of turning ch.

Row 7: Repeat Row 6. Drop one strand of A, change to B when 2 lps remain in final st at end of row.

Row 8: Ch 3, turn. Sk first dc. *LC in next dc, ch 1, sk 1 dc. Repeat from * across, working final LC in top of turning ch. Drop A, pick up C when 2 lps remain in final st at end of row.

Row 9: Ch 3, turn. Sk first LC. *LC in ch sp, ch 1, sk LC. Repeat from * across, working final LC in ch-3 sp. Drop B, pick up A when 2 lps remain in final st at end of row.

Row 10: Ch 3, turn. Sk first LC. *LC in ch sp, ch 1, sk LC. Repeat from * across, working final LC in ch-3 sp.

Drop C, pick up B when 2 lps remain in final st at end of row.

Row 11: Ch 1, turn. Sc in each st across. Fasten off.

FINISHING

Lightly steam block scarf on WS. With WS facing you, use yarn tails to sew seam closed. Weave in remaining ends.

Double-Strand Delight
Section of Pattern

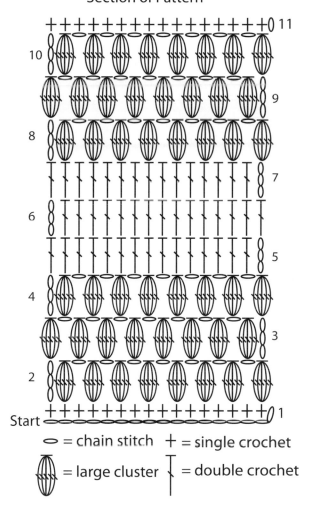

○ = chain stitch + = single crochet

= large cluster = double crochet

Firelight Turtleneck

The neck of this combination turtleneck-capelet is worked sideways to create ribbing, then the yoke is crocheted perpendicular to that. It's designed to fit equally well under or on top of a coat or blazer.

SKILL LEVEL

INTERMEDIATE

MEASUREMENTS

Neck height 7.25 in. (19 cm) unfolded, 3.5 in. (9 cm) when folded over; neck 11 in. (28 cm) from side to side when item is laid flat; bottom of capelet 17.5 in. (44.5 cm) from side to side when item is laid flat.

MATERIALS

Bulky

Lion Brand Unique (100% acrylic; 3.5 oz./100 g, 109 yd./100 m)

» Garden (211), 3 skeins

U.S. size J-10 (6.00 mm) crochet hook
Tapestry needle

GAUGE

11 stitches and 10 rows in neck pattern (hdc rows alternating with rows of sc in blo) = 4 in. (10.2 cm), blocked

For gauge swatch, ch 26 and follow pattern until swatch measures at least 4.5 in. (11.4 cm). If your gauge matches, use it as the first rows of the project.

Pattern

NECK

Ch 26. The last 2 chs count as the first hdc on Row 1.

Row 1 (WS): Hdc in third ch from hook and in each ch across. Total 24 hdc.

Row 2 (RS): Ch 1, turn. Sc in blo of hdc at base of ch and in each hdc across, ending with sc in top of ch-2. Total 24 sc.

Row 3: Ch 2, turn. Sk st at base of chs. Hdc in each st across. Total 24 hdc.

Repeat Rows 2 and 3 until fabric measures 19.5 in. (49.5 cm, approximately 57 rows), ending with Row 2. Do not fasten off.

Joining row: With RS together, insert hook into back loop of final ch from the foundation row. Sl st to join. *Insert hook in next st on final row and the corresponding ch from the foundation row. Sl st to join. Repeat from * to end of row. Do not fasten off. The seam will be hidden when you fold down the turtleneck.

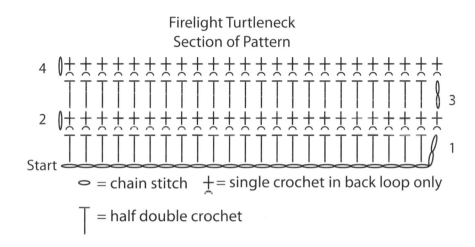

Firelight Turtleneck
Section of Pattern

○ = chain stitch   ┼ = single crochet in back loop only

┬ = half double crochet

YOKE

Notes: Make sure WS is facing out so that when you fold the turtleneck down, the ribbed side will show. The yoke is worked in rounds around the bottom circumference of the neck. Turn your work for each round as instructed.

Stitches on the yoke are worked in both loops, not the blo.

Row 1: Ch 1. Work 68 sc evenly around entire circumference of turtleneck. (*Tip: Mentally divide the round into quarters. Work 17 sc into each quarter to get the correct total.*) Join to ch-1 with sl st.

Row 2: Ch 3 (counts as dc here and throughout), turn. Sk the st at the base of the chs. Dc in each st around. Total 68 dc. Join to top of ch-3 with sl st.

Row 3 (begin increase): Ch 3, turn. Sk st at base of chs. Dc in each of next 2 sts, 2 dc in next st. *Dc in each of next 3 sts, 2 dc in next st. Repeat from *

around row, ending with 2 dc in final st. Total 85 dc. Join to top of ch-3 with sl st.

Row 4: Ch 3, turn. Sk st at base of chs. Dc in each st around. Total 85 dc. Join to ch-3 with sl st.

Row 5: Ch 3, turn. Sk st at base of chs. Dc in each of next 3 st, 2 dc in next st. *Dc in each of next 4 sts, 2 dc in next st. Repeat from * around until 4 sts remain. Dc in each remaining st. Total 100 dc. Join to ch-3 with sl st.

Row 6: Ch 3, turn. Sk st at base of chs. Dc in each st around. Total 100 dc. Join to ch-3 with sl st.

Row 7: Ch 1, turn. Sc in each st around. Join to ch-1 with sl st. Fasten off.

FINISHING

Weave in ends. Lightly steam block on WS if desired.

Firelight Turtleneck
Section of Yoke

○ = chain stitch

+ = single crochet

⊤ = double crochet

V = double crochet 2 in same stitch

• = slip stitch

▨ = repeat stitches

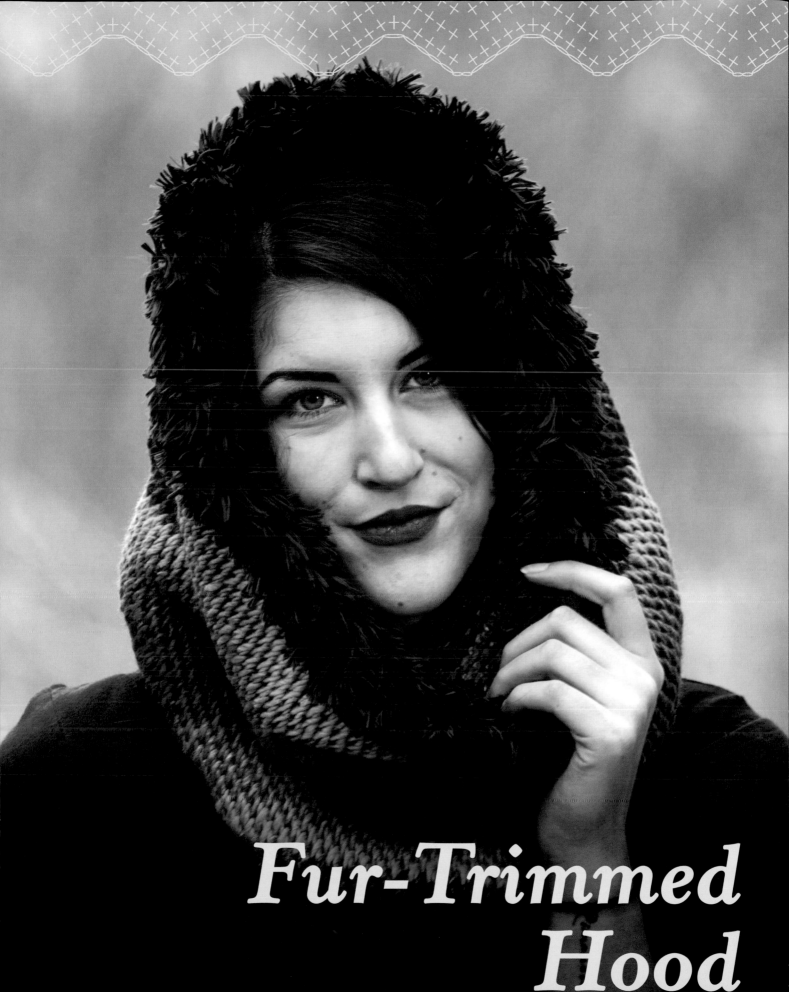

Fur-Trimmed
Hood

*W*ear this cowl gathered around your neck or extended as a hood. Either way, you'll love the rich colors and interesting texture of Tunisian full stitch worked in the round. Faux fur trim finishes off this fabulous accessory.

SKILL LEVEL

INTERMEDIATE

MEASUREMENTS
16 in. (10.5 cm) by 31 in. (78.75 cm) in circumference

MATERIALS

 5 **Bulky**   **7** **JUMBO**

Yarn A: Crystal Palace Yarns Danube Bulky (40% nylon, 30% wool, 30% rayon; 1.75 oz./50 g, 81 yd./74 m)

» Candy Store (909), 5 balls

Yarn B: Red Heart Boutique Fur (100% polyester; 3.5 oz./100 g, 11 yd./10 m)

» Eggplant (9554), 1 ball

U.S. size K-10½ (6.5 mm) double-ended Tunisian crochet hook connected by flexible plastic piece; total length from one hook tip to the other should be at least 23 in. (58.3 cm)
Stitch marker
Tapestry needle

GAUGE
13 stitches and 15 rows in Tfs/4 in. (10.2 cm), blocked

Special Stitch

Tunisian Full Stitch
(sometimes called Tunisian Net Stitch)

Forward pass: Insert hook from front to back in the space between two stitches, yo, pull up lp. Be sure to go through the space, not through the "legs" within a stitch.

Return pass: The return pass is worked in the same direction as the forward pass, except it's done on the inside of the piece. Follow instructions in Pattern for doing the return pass in the round.

Pattern Notes

» You will need to work from two balls of yarn at the same time, one for the forward pass and one for the return. After you use up four balls of yarn, divide the fifth ball of yarn in half to make the final two balls.

» The first two rows are worked in standard single crochet. Tunisian crochet rounds begin on Row 3. The rounds are worked in spiral fashion.

Pattern

With A and double-ended Tunisian hook, ch 101.
Note: You will only use one end of the hook on Rows 1 and 2.

Row 1: Sc in second ch from hook and in each ch across. Total 100 sc.

Row 2: Ch 1, turn. Sc in each sc across.

Round 3 (begin Tunisian crochet): Turn. Do not ch 1. The loop on hook counts as first st. Place stitch marker on that stitch to indicate the beginning of the round. *Enter next st as for sc, yo, pull up lp (counts as Tunisian knit stitch). Repeat from * until you have around 30 lps on the hook (exact number does not matter).

Rotate the project 180 degrees. Slide the stitches to the other end of the hook. You will be looking at the WS (the inside) of the cowl.

With new ball of A, yo, pull through 1 lp. *Yo, pull through 2 lps. Repeat from * until 4 lps remain on hook. This is the return pass. (You can think of it as "chasing" the forward pass on the inside of the cowl.)

NOTE: *Only the first stitch at the beginning of the first return pass is "yo, pull through 1 lp." All subsequent return pass stitches, including the first stitch every time you turn the hook to begin the return pass stitches, are "yo, pull through 2 lps."*

Rotate project back the other way, slide the stitches to the other end of the hook, and continue the forward pass. When you get to the end of the forward pass on Round 3, continue forward on Row 4 with Tfs. Move marker to the first st on Round 4.

Round 4–end: Continue to work around the cowl a bit at a time in spiral fashion, working Tfs between each pair of sts until you have a comfortable number on your hook, then rotating the piece to work the return pass for the stitches you have made. Always leave at least 3 lps between the return pass and the forward pass so that your return pass does not overtake the forward pass. Move the marker up every time you complete a round. Each round should have 100 stitches. Add a new ball of yarn when you have about 4 in. (10.2 cm) left on the current ball. You will have to do this for the forward and the return pass.

When your yarn is almost used up, work the forward pass until the last st before the marker. This should place you exactly above the starting point from Row 1, which is at the center back of the cowl. (If you do not have enough yarn to complete the round, stop at the end of the previous round. I got 57 rounds of Tfs.) Fasten off the forward pass yarn. Complete the return pass and fasten off that yarn.

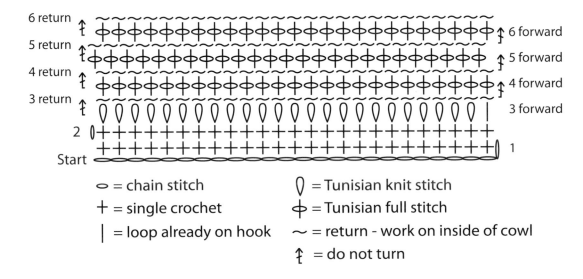

Fur-Trimmed Hood
Section of Pattern

○ = chain stitch
+ = single crochet
| = loop already on hook
Ω = Tunisian knit stitch
φ = Tunisian full stitch
~ = return - work on inside of cowl
↕ = do not turn

FINISHING AND TRIM

Turn cowl WS out. With beginning tail, seam Rows 1 and 2 closed. Weave in remaining ends.

Turn cowl RS out. Join B at center back. Ch 1, sc in next sp (where the next Tfs would be). *Sk 1 sp, sc in next sp. Repeat from * around. Join to ch with sl st. Fasten off. Weave in ends of B.

Lightly steam block main part of cowl on WS if desired. Do not steam the fur.

Fur-Trimmed Hood
Section of Trim

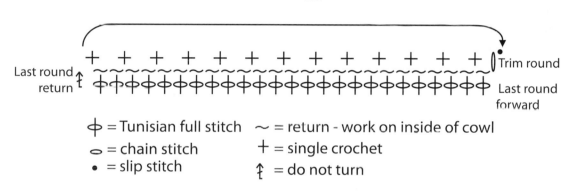

Φ = Tunisian full stitch   ~ = return - work on inside of cowl

○ = chain stitch   + = single crochet

• = slip stitch   ↕ = do not turn

Green Fields Capelet

Gorgeous green yarn with flecks of gold is shown off to great advantage with the variety of Tunisian stitches in this capelet. Fringe around the bottom (crocheted in loop stitch—no need to tie on each strand separately!) adds even more flair.

SKILL LEVEL

EXPERIENCED

MEASUREMENTS

28 in. (71 cm) neckline circumference, 39 in. (99 cm) bottom circumference, 11 in. (28 cm) from neckline to bottom of fringe

MATERIALS

Light

Blue Heron Yarns Rayon Metallic (88% rayon, 12% metallic; 8 oz./227 g, 550 yd./503 m)

» Lemon-Lime, 1 skein

U.S. size J-10 (6.0 mm) Tunisian crochet hook
Tapestry needle

GAUGE

20 stitches and 15 rows in pattern = 4 in. (10.2 cm), blocked.

For gauge swatch, ch 30.

Row 1: Insert hook into second ch from hook, yo, pull up lp. *Insert hook into next ch, pull up lp. Repeat from * across. Total 30 lps on hook. Return.

Row 2: Sk first two vertical bars, Tss in next vertical bar. Working in front of st just made, Tss in the second skipped vertical bar (the one immediately before the one where you just made the Tss). To make it easier to find the skipped vertical bar, gently stretch the work vertically. *Move to next pair

of unworked vertical bars. Sk next vertical bar, Tss in following vertical bar. Working in front of st just made, Tss in skipped vertical bar. Repeat from * across, ending with Tss in last vertical bar. Return. Repeat Row 2 until swatch measures at least 4.5 in. (11.4 cm).

Special Stitches

Tunisian Simple Stitch 2 Together (Tss2tog)
Slide hook through vertical bars of next 2 sts, yo, pull up lp.

1. Insert hook as for sc.

2. Using a finger of your free hand, pull up the yarn to form a loop approximately 1 in. (2.5 cm) tall.

3. Put hook behind both strands of the loop near the base and pull up both strands, leaving the loopy end sticking out the back.

4. Release the loop from your finger. Using working yarn (not tall loop), yo and pull through all 3 loops.

Pattern

Ch 180.

Row 1: Insert hook into second ch from hook, yo, pull up lp. *Insert hook into next ch, pull up lp. Repeat from * across. Total 180 lps on hook. Return.

Row 2: Sk first two vertical bars, Tss in next vertical bar. Working in front of st just made, Tss in the second skipped vertical bar (the one immediately before the one where you just made the Tss). To make it easier to find the skipped vertical bar, gently stretch the work between your thumbs. *Move to next pair of unworked vertical bars. Sk next vertical bar, Tss in following vertical bar. Working in front of st just made, Tss in skipped vertical bar. Repeat from * across, ending with Tss in last vertical bar. Return.

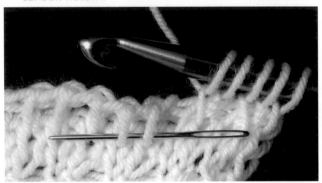

Rows 3–7: Repeat Row 2.

Row 8: Sk first vertical bar. *Insert hook in next 2 vertical bars, yo, pull through both to add 1 lp to hook, yo to add another lp. Repeat from * across, ending with Tss in final vertical bar. Return.

Row 9: Sk first vertical bar. Tss in next vertical bar. *Tfs in next sp (insert hook from front to back through sp, yo, pull up lp), Tss in next vertical bar. Repeat from * across, ending with Tss in final vertical bar. Return.

Rows 10–13: Repeat Rows 8 and 9 twice.

Row 14: Sk first vertical bar. *Tps in next vertical bar, Tss in next vertical bar. Repeat from * across, ending with Tps in final vertical bar. Return.

Row 15: Sk first vertical bar. *Tss in next st, Tps in next st. (The stitches are staggered: work a Tss into the Tps from the previous row, and a Tps into the Tss from the previous row. This creates the honeycomb.) Repeat from * across, ending with Tss in final vertical bar. Return.

Rows 16–19: Repeat Rows 14 and 15 twice.

Rows 20–25: Repeat Rows 8 and 9 three times.

Row 26: Sk first vertical bar. Tss in each remaining st across. Return.

BEGIN SHOULDER SHAPING

Row 27: Sk first vertical bar. Work 6 Tss, Tss2tog. *Work 9 Tss, Tss2tog. Repeat from * to last 6 sts. Tss in each remaining st. Return. Total 164 sts.

Row 28: Sk first vertical bar. Work 3 Tss, Tss2tog. *Work 4 Tss, Tss2tog. Repeat from * across to last 2 sts. Tss in each remaining st. Return. Total 137 sts.

Row 29: Sk first vertical bar. Work 3 Tss, Tss2tog. *Work 4 Tss, Tss2tog. Repeat from * across to last 5 sts. Tss in each remaining st. Return. Total 115 sts.

Rows 30–34: Sk first vertical bar. Tss in each st across. Return.

Row 35: Sk first vertical bar. Work 11 Tss, Tss2tog. *Work 12 Tss, Tss2tog. Repeat from * until 3 sts remain. Tss in each remaining st. Return. Total 107 sts.

Row 36: Sk first vertical bar. Tss in each st across. Return.

Note: Ordinarily, I like to finish Tunisian crochet garments with a row of single crochet. Here I chose not to, in order to take advantage of Tunisian simple stitch's natural curl, creating a nice roll-neck.

FINISHING

Lightly steam block on WS if desired.

With WS facing you, sew back seam closed. Make sure stitch patterns are lined up. Weave in ends.

Fringe

With WS facing, join yarn at bottom of back seam. Ch 1. Working into the unused loops of the foundation ch, lp st in each st across. Fasten off.

Turn RS out. Snip the bottom of each loop to create fringe. Trim if necessary to make fringe even. Lightly steam block if desired.

Green Fields Capelet
Section of Pattern

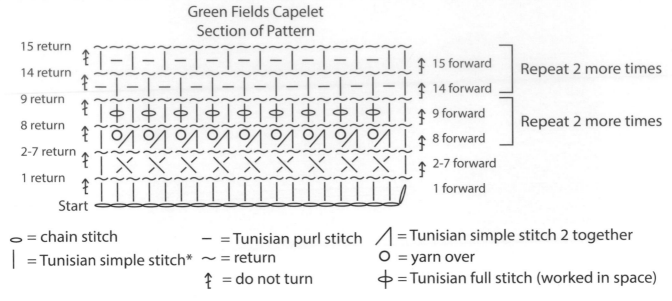

o = chain stitch   − = Tunisian purl stitch   ╱| = Tunisian simple stitch 2 together

| = Tunisian simple stitch*   ~ = return   O = yarn over

↕ = do not turn   ⏁ = Tunisian full stitch (worked in space)

╳ = Working in pair of unworked vertical bars, sk next vertical bar, Tss in following vertical bar. Working in front of st just made, Tss in skipped vertical bar.

When this symbol is the first stitch in the row, it represents the loop already on the hook.

Green Fields Capelet
Section of Shoulder Shaping

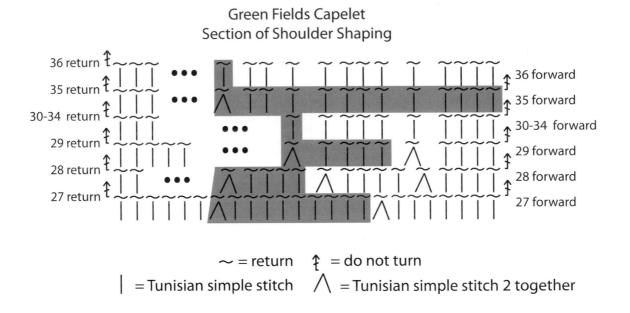

~ = return   ↕ = do not turn

| = Tunisian simple stitch   ∧ = Tunisian simple stitch 2 together

••• = repeat shaded area until last stitches shown

Green Fields Capelet
Section of Fringe

♡ = loop stitch   • = slip stitch

o = chain stitch (unworked loops of foundation chain)

Intarsia Arrows

*W*hat's black, white, and red all over? This stylish intarsia cowl, worked flat in Tunisian crochet and then seamed. Using two colors in any given row for the center section, the working color is pulled up in the right spot to match the pattern, with the unused color carried across the back.

SKILL LEVEL

INTERMEDIATE

MEASUREMENTS
6.5 in. (16.5 cm) by 21 in. (53.5 cm) in circumference

MATERIALS

Light

Plymouth Yarn Baby Alpaca Cherish (50% baby alpaca, 50% acrylic, 1.75 oz./50 g, 136 yd./125 m

» Color A: Red Moon (23), 1 ball
» Color B: Black (32), 1 ball
» Color C: White (10), 1 ball

U.S. size H-8 (5.0 mm) Tunisian crochet hook for bottom and top ribbing
U.S. size I-9 (5.5 mm) Tunisian crochet hook for intarsia section
Tapestry needle

GAUGE
23 stitches and 17 rows in Tss intarsia = 4 in. (10.2 cm), blocked

Special Stitches

Tunisian Simple Stitch Into Foundation Chain
1. Insert hook where indicated. Yarn over, pull up a loop.

Tunisian Purl Stitch Into Foundation Chain
1. Bring the yarn to the front of the work.

2. Insert the hook into the second chain from the hook.

3. Let the yarn go. Bring it toward you in front of the stitch, then back under the hook.

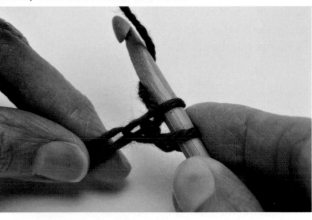

4. Yarn over, pull up a loop with that yarn. There will be two loops on the hook.

5. Continue in this fashion all the way across, adding a loop to the hook with each stitch. Notice the "purl bump" in the front of each stitch. Count the loops—you should have the same number as the foundation chain.

6. Do not turn. Work standard return (yo, pull through 1 lp, *yo, pull through 2 lps, repeat from * until 1 lp remains on hook).

Special Techniques

Intarsia (Stranded Colorwork)
You'll be changing colors as you work the forward pass. Carry the yarn loosely across the wrong side. On the return pass, change to new color when the second loop you'll pull through is the new color.

To keep the yarn from tangling, pull the colors into position the same way each time. For example, pull B over C, and C under B. If necessary, stop and rearrange your balls of yarn so the strands don't get twisted.

When the first stitch of the next row is a different color than the last stitch on the return pass being completed, work the final stitch with the color of the next row.

Pattern Notes

» For step-by-step instructions on how to work the Tunisian simple stitch and Tunisian purl stitch, see pages 96–100.

Pattern

With A and smaller hook, ch 126.

Row 1: Tss in second ch from hook. *Tps in each of next 3 chs, Tss in each of next 2 chs. Repeat from * across until 1 st remains. Tss in final st. Return.

Rows 2–5: Tss in second st from hook. *Tps in each of next 3 sts, Tss in each of next 2 sts. Repeat from * across until 1 st remains. Tss in final st. Return. Change to B when 2 lps remain on hook at end of Row 5 return. Cut A, leaving about a 4-inch (10.2 cm) tail.

Note: Switch to larger hook for intarsia section. All stitches are worked in Tunisian simple stitch.

Rows 6–22: Follow intarsia chart, changing colors as indicated. Remember to change color in the final return stitch of Rows 6, 9, 12, 15, 18, and 21 because the first stitch of the subsequent row is in the new color.

Change to A when 2 sts remain on hook at the end of the Row 22 return pass. Cut B and C, leaving about a 4-inch (10.2 cm) tail for each.

Note: Switch back to smaller hook for top ribbing.

Row 23: Tss in each st across. Return.

Rows 24–27: Repeat Row 2.

Row 28: Sc in each st across, entering each stitch as for Tss or Tps to remain in pattern. Fasten off.

FINISHING

Lightly steam block on WS.

With the RS facing you, line up the ends so the pattern matches. Using matching yarn, sew a flat seam. Weave in any remaining ends.

Intarsia Arrows
Section of Pattern

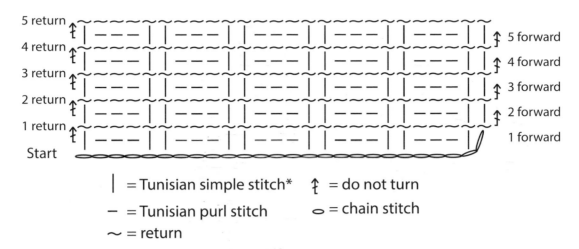

| | = Tunisian simple stitch*   ↕ = do not turn

−   = Tunisian purl stitch   ○ = chain stitch

~   = return

When this symbol is the first stitch in the row, it represents the loop already on the hook.

Intarsia Arrows
Section of Pattern

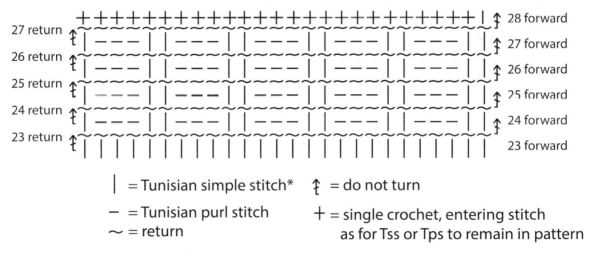

| | = Tunisian simple stitch*   ↕ = do not turn

−   = Tunisian purl stitch   + = single crochet, entering stitch
~   = return   as for Tss or Tps to remain in pattern

When this symbol is the first stitch in the row, it represents the loop already on the hook.

Intarsia Arrows
Center Section of Pattern - Intarsia Diagram
Note: All stitches are Tunisian simple stitch

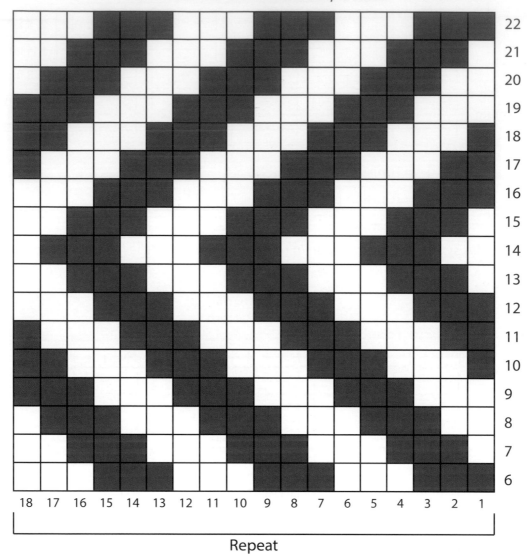

Repeat

■ = Color B   ☐ = Color C

Loopy
Boa

*M*ake a statement and stay warm at the same time with this lavish loop stitch neck warmer.

SKILL LEVEL

INTERMEDIATE

MEASUREMENTS

14 in. (35.5 cm) around short way of tube by 45 in. (104 cm) in circumference

MATERIALS

Medium

Bernat Satin (100% acrylic; 3.5 oz./100 g, 200 yd./ 182 m)

» Color A: Ebony (04040), 2 skeins
» Color B: Snow (04005), 2 skeins
» Color C: Grey Mist Heather (04045), 2 skeins

U.S. size I-9 (5.5 mm) crochet hook
Tapestry needle

GAUGE

13 stitches and 8 rows in pattern = 4 in. (10.2 cm), blocked

For gauge swatch, ch 24. Last 3 chs count as first dc on Row 1.

Row 1 (RS): Dc in fourth ch from hook and in each ch across. Total 22 dc.

Row 2 (WS): Ch 1, turn. Work lp st in each st across. Total 22 lp sts.

Row 3: Ch 3, turn. Sk st at base of chs. Dc in each remaining st across (do not work a st in the turning ch). Total 22 dc.

Row 4: Ch 1, turn. Work lp st in each st across. Total 22 lp sts.

Repeat Rows 3 and 4 until swatch measures at least 4.5 in. (11.4 cm).

Special Stitch

Loop Stitch (lp st)

Note: Loop stitches are worked on WS rows because the loops form at the back of the fabric and will appear on the RS.

1. Insert hook as for single crochet.

2. Using a finger of your free hand, pull up the yarn to form a loop approximately 1 in. (2.5 cm) tall.

3. Put hook behind both strands of the loop near the base and pull up both strands, leaving the loopy end sticking out the back.

4. Release the loop from your finger. Using working yarn (not tall loop), yo and pull through all 3 loops.

Pattern Notes

» Cowl is seamed the long way and then the short ends are joined to form a tube.

» Loop stitches are worked on WS rows because the loops form at the back of the fabric and will appear on the RS. The RS rows in this pattern are worked in double crochet.

Pattern

With A, ch 46. Last 3 chs count as first dc on Row 1.

Row 1 (RS): Dc in fourth ch from hook and in each ch across. Total 44 dc.

Row 2 (WS): Ch 1, turn. Work lp st in each st across. Total 44 lp sts.

Row 3: Ch 3, turn. Sk st at base of chs. Dc in each remaining st across (do not work a st in the turning ch). Total 44 dc.

Row 4: Ch 1, turn. Row 2 (WS): Ch 1, turn. Work lp st in each st across. Total 44 lp sts.

Rows 5–10: Repeat Rows 3 and 4 three times. Change to B when 2 sts remain at the end of Row 10. Cut A.

Rows 11–20: Repeat Rows 3 and 4 five times. Change to C when 2 sts remain at the end of Row 20. Cut B.

Rows 21–30: Repeat Rows 3 and 4 five times. Change to A when 2 sts remain at the end of Row 30. Cut C.

Rows 31–40: Repeat Rows 3 and 4 five times. Change to B when 2 sts remain at the end of Row 40. Cut A.

Rows 41–50: Repeat Rows 3 and 4 five times. Change to C when 2 sts remain at the end of Row 50. Cut B.

Rows 51–60: Repeat Rows 3 and 4 five times. Change to A when 2 sts remain at the end of Row 60. Cut C.

Rows 61–90: Repeat Rows 31–60. Do not change colors at end of Row 90. Fasten off.

FINISHING

Weave in ends. With WS (flat side, not loopy side) facing you, seam the long ends together. Be careful to match up the rows and not to catch any loops from the other side into your seam.

Turn RS out. Seam the two ends together to complete the circle. Make sure you do not sew the tube closed as you make the seam.

Loopy Boa
Section of Pattern

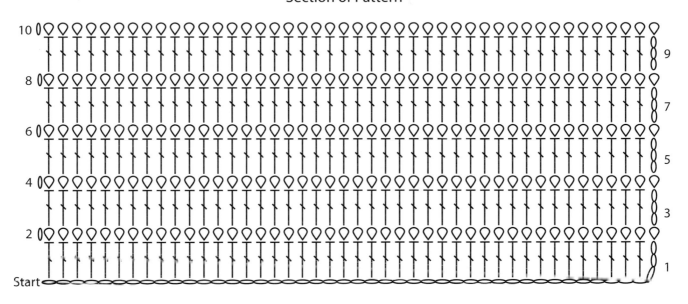

◯ = chain stitch ♡ = loop stitch ‖ = double crochet

Magenta
Mosaic

*M*osaic crochet, in which one color is worked several rows below to cover the in-between color, makes distinctive lozenge shapes.

SKILL LEVEL

INTERMEDIATE

MEASUREMENTS

9 in. (23 cm) by 24 in. (61 cm) in circumference

MATERIALS

Super Fine

Madelintosh Tosh Merino Light (100% superwash merino wool; 3.5 oz./100 g; 420 yd./384 m)

» Color A: Leopard, 1 skein
» Color B: Fluoro Rose, 1 skein

U.S. size E-4 (3.5 mm) crochet hook
Tapestry needle

GAUGE

21 stitches and 12 rows in dc = 4 in. (10.2 cm), blocked

For gauge swatch, ch 35. Last 3 chs count as first dc on Row 1.

Row 1: Dc into fourth ch from hook and in each ch across. Total 33 dc.

Row 2: Ch 3 (counts as dc), turn. Sk st at base of chs. Dc in each st across, ending with final dc in top of turning ch. Total 33 dc.

Repeat Row 2 until swatch measures at least 4.5 in. (11.4 cm)

Lightly steam block your swatch and measure your gauge.

Special Stitch

Lozenge Mosaic

With A, ch multiple of 12 plus 11. (For a practice swatch, ch 35.)

Row 1: Sc into second ch from hook and in each ch to end. (Swatch will have 34 sc.)

Row 2: Ch 1, turn. Sc in each st across, changing to B when 2 lps remain on hook in final st. Cut A.

Note: On the cowl, not the swatch, you will be sewing the ends together along this edge, so it is better to cut the yarn than to carry it along the seam. When you finish the project you can use the tails to sew the two sides together—lining up the colors perfectly. Leave about a 4-inch (10.2 cm) tail when you cut the yarn so you can thread it through a tapestry needle for the seam.

Row 3: With B, ch 3 (counts as dc), turn. Sk sc at base of chs. Dc into next sc, hdc into next sc, sc into next sc. *Ch 2, sk 2 sc. Sc into next sc, hdc into next sc, dc into each of next 2 sc, tr into each of next 2 sc, dc into each of next 2 sc, hdc into next sc, sc into next sc. Repeat from * to last 6 sc. Ch 2, sk 2 sc. Sc into next sc, hdc into next sc, dc into each of next 2 sc.

Note: This sets up the wave pattern. From the small end, each lozenge consists of 10 stitches: sc, hdc, dc, dc, tr, tr, dc, dc, hdc, sc on this row. The lozenges are separated by 2 chs (skipping over 2 stitches below). On the next row, you will reinforce those stitches: sc will be worked into sc from the row below, hdc will be worked into hdc from the row below, etc.

Row 4: Ch 3, turn. Sk dc at base of chs. Dc in next dc, hdc in next hdc, sc in next sc. *Ch 2, sk 2 ch. Sc into next sc, hdc into next hdc, dc into each of next 2 dc, tr into each of next 2 tr, dc into each of next 2 dc, hdc into next hdc, sc into next sc. Repeat from * to last 6 sc. Ch 2, sk 2 ch. Sc into next sc, hdc into next hdc, dc into next dc, dc into top of turning ch, changing to A when 2 lps remain on hook in final st. Cut B.

Row 5: With A, ch 1, turn. Sc into each of next 4 sts. Sc into each of 2 unworked sc from 3 rows below, inserting hook from the front and pulling the lp up to the same height as the current row. *Sc into each of next sts, sc into each of 2 unworked sc from 3 rows below. Repeat from * until 4 sts remain. Sc into each of next 3 sts, sc into top of turning ch.

Row 6: Ch 1, turn. Sc into each sc across, changing to B when 2 lps remain on hook in final st. Cut A.

Row 7: With B, ch 1, turn. *Sc in sc, hdc in next sc, dc in each of next 2 sc, tr in each of next 2 sc, dc in each of next 2 sc, hdc in next sc, sc in next sc. Ch 2, sk 2 sc. Repeat from * across, omitting ch 2 at end of row.

Row 8: Ch 1, turn. *Sc in sc, hdc in hdc, dc in each of next 2 dc, tr in each of next 2 tr, dc in each of next 2 dc, hdc in hdc, sc in sc. Ch 2, sk 2 ch below. Repeat from * across, omitting ch 2 at end of row. Change to A when 2 lps remain on hook. Cut B.

Row 9: With A, ch 1, turn. *Sc in each of the next 10 sts. Sc into each of 2 unworked sc from 3 rows below, inserting hook from the front and pulling the lp up to the same height as the current row. Repeat from * across, omitting 2 sc at end of row.

Repeat Rows 2–9.

Pattern

With A, ch 143. *To make the circumference of the cowl larger, add stitches in a multiple of 12.*

Row 1 (RS): Sc into second ch from hook and in each ch across. Total 142 sc.

Rows 2–49: Work Rows 2–9 of Lozenge Mosaic pattern six times.

Row 50: Ch 1, turn. Sc in each st across. Fasten off.

FINISHING

Lightly steam block scarf on WS. Do not weave in ends.

With RS together so WS is facing you, bring short ends of cowl together. Thread one of the tails onto a tapestry needle and stitch to the corresponding end of the cowl, matching up the color. Weave in the end. Repeat the process with remaining tails. Keep seam as flat as possible. It will be almost invisible when you're done. *Note: Where the sc stitches meet in Color B, sew together with A to match the sc spike stitches in the body of the cowl.*

Weave in any remaining ends. Invert the cowl so the RS faces out.

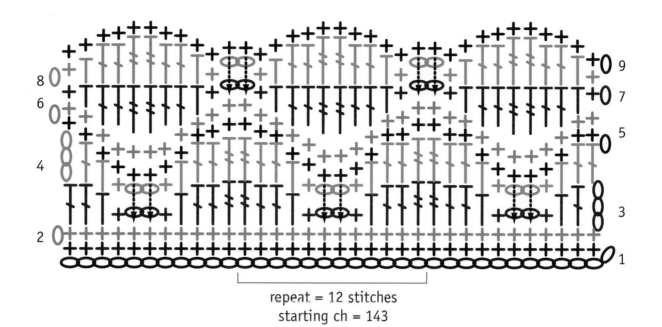

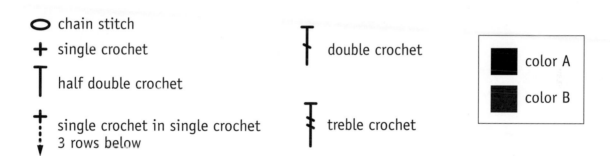

repeat = 12 stitches
starting ch = 143

⬭ chain stitch

✚ single crochet

╤ half double crochet

┇ single crochet in single crochet
↓ 3 rows below

╤ double crochet

╪ treble crochet

| | color A |
| | color B |

Maritime
Chevrons

*T*here's something crisp and efficient about chevrons. You can wear this cowl long or loop it around a second time for a different look. Either way, you're likely to feel an instant confidence boost when you don this tidy scarf.

SKILL LEVEL

EASY +

MEASUREMENTS
5.25 in. (13.25 cm) by 52 in. (132 cm), before seaming

MATERIALS

Fine

Plymouth Yarn Galway Sport (100% Highland wool; 1.75 oz./50 g, 151 yd./138 m)

» Color A: Indigo (0185), 2 skeins
» Color B: Natural (0001), 1 skein

U.S. size G-7 (4.5 mm) crochet hook
Tapestry needle

GAUGE
25 stitches and 14 rows in chevron pattern = 4 in. (10.2 cm), blocked
For gauge, follow the pattern instructions until your swatch measures at least 4.5 in. (11.4 cm). If your gauge matches, you can simply continue with the cowl.

Pattern Notes

» The chevron stitch is made by working 3 sc in one st at the apex of the chevron and skipping 2 sts to create a trough at the base.

Pattern

With A, ch 35.

Row 1 (RS): Work 2 sc in second ch from hook. *Sc into each of next 4 chs, sk 2 chs, sc into each of next 4 chs, 3 sc into next ch. Repeat from * ending last rep with 2 sc into last ch.

Row 2: Ch 1 (does not count as st), turn. Work 2 sc into first st. *Sc into each of next 4 sts, sk 2 sts, sc into each of next 4 sts, 3 sc into next st. Repeat from * ending last rep with 2 sc into last st.

Rows 3–4: Repeat Row 2, changing to B when 2 lps remain on hook at end of Row 4. Do not cut A.

Note: Carry A up the side, making sure it is snug but not overly tight when you start working with it again.

Rows 5–6: With B, repeat Row 2, changing to A when 2 lps remain on hook at end of Row 6. Cut B.

Note: You may cut or carry B. I find it neater to cut it, leaving about a 4-inch (10.2 cm) tail, and start a new yarn the next time the pattern calls for B. If you carry the yarn, there will be fewer ends to weave in later, but make sure it goes neatly up the side and doesn't cause the cowl to pucker.

Rows 7–180: Continue to work 4 rows in A, 2 rows in B, until there are 30 sections of each color. Fasten off B. Cut A, leaving an 8-inch (20.25 cm) tail.

FINISHING AND TRIM

Lightly steam block on WS. Using tapestry needle, weave in all ends except for the final tail.

With WS facing you, sew beginning and end together with the tail of B.

Turn RS out. Join A on one side at seam. Ch 1. Sc evenly around. Join to ch-1 with sl st. Fasten off. Repeat for other side. Weave in ends.

Maritime Chevrons
Section of Pattern

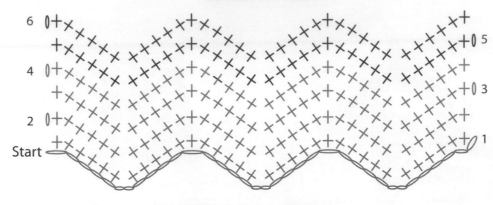

○ = chain stitch   ⬛ = Color A   ⬛ = Color B

+ = single crochet

x+ = 2 single crochet in same stitch

x+x = 3 single crochet in same stitch

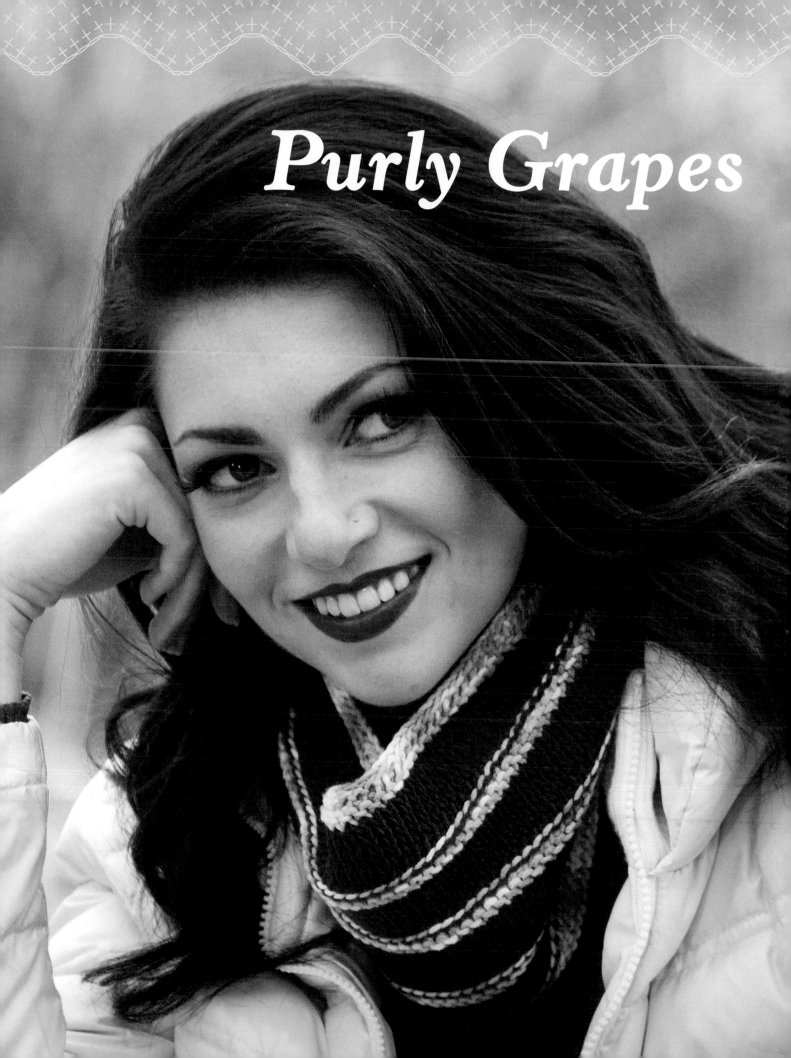

Purly Grapes

*S*olid bands of Tunisian knit stitch alternate with colorful
rows of Tunisian purl.

SKILL LEVEL

EASY

MEASUREMENTS
6.5 in. (16.5 cm) by 24 in. (61 cm) in circumference

MATERIALS

Light

Crystal Palace Yarns Cuddles DK (100% microfiber
acrylic; 1.75 oz./50 g, 131 yd./120 m)

» Color A: Delicate (2003), 1 ball
» Color B: Byzantium (114), 2 balls

U.S. size H-10½ (5.0 mm) Tunisian crochet hook
Tapestry needle

GAUGE
16 stitches and 17 rows in Tks/4 in. (10.2 cm), blocked

Special Stitches

Tunisian Purl Stitch Into Foundation Chain

1. Bring the yarn to the front of the work.

2. Insert the hook into the second chain from the hook.

3. Let the yarn go. Bring it toward you in front of the stitch, then back under the hook.

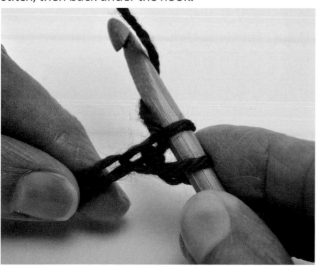

4. Yarn over, pull up a loop with that yarn. There will be two loops on the hook.

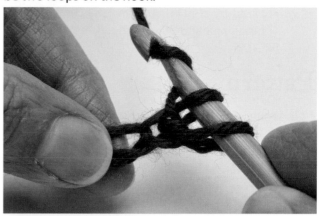

5. Continue in this fashion all the way across, adding a loop to the hook with each stitch. Notice the "purl bump" in the front of each stitch. Count the loops—you should have the same number as the foundation chain.

6. Do not turn. Work standard return (yo, pull through 1 lp, *yo, pull through 2 lps, repeat from * until 1 lp remains on hook).

Pattern Notes

» For step-by-step instructions on how to work Tunisian knit and purl stitches, see pages 97–100.

Pattern

Note: When you switch to a new color, cut the old yarn, leaving a 4-inch (10.2 cm) tail.

With A, ch 105. *To make a looser cowl, add stitches to the initial chain (4 stitches for each additional inch). Every row will have that number of stitches.*

Row 1: Tps in second ch from hook and in each ch across. Return.

Row 2: Sk first vertical bar. Tps in each st across. Return, changing to B when 2 lps remain at end of Row 2 return.

Row 3: Sk first vertical bar. Tks in each st across, being sure to insert the hook above the purl bump. Return.

Rows 4–8: Sk first vertical bar. Tks in each st across. Return, changing to A when 2 lps remain at end of Row 8 return.

Row 9: Sk first vertical bar. Tps in each st across. Return.

Row 10: Sk first vertical bar. Tps in each st across. Return, changing to B when 2 lps remain at end of Row 10 return.

Rows 11–32: Repeat Rows 3–10 twice, then Rows 3–8 once. Change to A when 2 lps remain at end of Row 32 return.

Row 33: Sk first vertical bar. Tps in each st across. Return.

Row 34: Sk first vertical bar. *Enter next st as for Tps, but pull through both lps to make a sl st. (You will not be adding lps onto the hook.) Repeat from * across. Fasten off.

FINISHING AND TRIM

Gently steam block on WS to ease any curl.

With WS facing you, use the yarn tails to seam closed. Keep the colors lined up. Weave in ends.

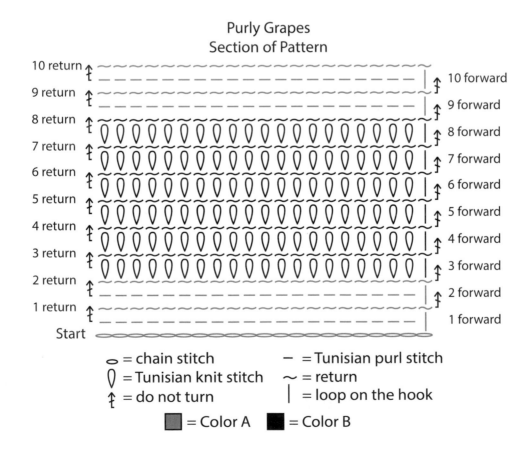

Purly Grapes
Section of Pattern

○ = chain stitch   — = Tunisian purl stitch
Ո = Tunisian knit stitch   ~ = return
↟ = do not turn | = loop on the hook

■ = Color A   ■ = Color B

Purly Grapes
Final Rows

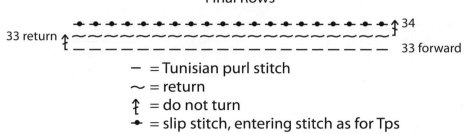

33 return

34

33 forward

− = Tunisian purl stitch

~ = return

↕ = do not turn

•— = slip stitch, entering stitch as for Tps

Zigzag Pip Stitch Cowl

*B*lue and white spots play peek-a-boo against a black background in this simple cowl. The trick is working two double crochet stitches together so they are joined at the top but have their bases in separate stitches.

The Ultimate Sourcebook of Knitting and Crochet Stitches calls this stitch pattern "Zigzag Pip." I couldn't possibly improve on that charming term!

SKILL LEVEL

INTERMEDIATE

MEASUREMENTS

5.5 in. (14 cm) by 49 in. (124.5 cm) in circumference

MATERIALS

Medium

Lion Brand Yarn LB Collection Crepe Twist (88% merino wool, 12% nylon; 1.75 oz./50 g; 112 yd./ 102 m)

» Color A: Royal (109), 1 skein
» Color B: Black (153), 3 skeins
» Color C: White (100), 1 skein

U.S. size H-8 (5 mm) crochet hook
Tapestry needle

GAUGE

17 stitches and 12 rows in pattern = 4 in. (10.2 cm), blocked

For gauge swatch, ch 30. Follow instructions for pattern below until swatch measures at least 4.5 in. (11.4 cm). Dc2tog counts as 1 st; ch sp counts as 1 st.

Special Stitch

Double Crochet 2 Together (dc2tog)
This takes two double crochet stitches and joins them
into one at the top.
Yo, insert hook where instructed, yo, pull up lp, yo,
    pull through 2 lps (2 lps remain on hook). Yo, insert
    hook where instructed, yo, pull up lp, yo, pull
    through 2 lps, yo, pull through remaining 3 lps.

Color Sequence

Note: When you change colors, cut the old color, leaving
    about a 4-inch (10.2 cm) tail.
The color progression is as follows:
Row 1: A
Row 2: B
Row 3: C
Row 4: B
Row 5: A
Row 6: B
Row 7: C
Row 8: B

Row 9: A
Row 10: B
Row 11: C
Row 12: B
Row 13: A
Row 14: B
Row 15: C
Row 16: B
Row 17: A

Pattern

With A, ch 202.
Row 1: Sc into second ch from hook. *Ch 1, sk 1 ch,
    sc into next ch. Repeat from * across, changing to
    B when 2 lps remain on hook at end of final st.
Row 2: Ch 3, turn. Dc into ch sp. (The ch-3 and the dc
    count as a dc2tog.) *Ch 1, dc2tog inserting hook
    into same sp as previous st for first leg and into
    next sp for second leg. Repeat from * to last sp,
    ending with ch 1, dc2tog over same sp and last sc.
    Do not work in turning ch. Change to C when 2 lps
    remain on hook at end of final st.

Row 3: Ch 1, turn. Sc into first st. *Sc into next sp, ch 1, sk next dc2tog. Repeat from * across ending with sc in last sp, sc in last stitch. Do not work in turning ch. Change to B when 2 lps remain on hook at end of final st.

Row 4: Ch 3, turn. Dc2tog inserting hook into first st (at base of chs) for first leg and into next sp for second leg. *Ch 1, dc2tog inserting hook into same sp as previous st for first leg and into next sp for second leg. Repeat from * across, ending with second leg of last dc2tog in last sc, dc into same place. Do not work in turning ch. Change to A when 2 lps remain on hook at end of final st.

Row 5: Ch 1, turn. Sc into first st. *Ch 1, sk next dc2tog, sc into next sp. Repeat from * across, working last sc into top of turning ch. Change to B when 2 lps remain on hook at end of final st.

Rows 6–17: Repeat Rows 2–5 three times. Do not change color at end of Row 17. Fasten off.

FINISHING

Lightly steam block on WS. Do not weave in ends.
With WS facing you, bring short ends of cowl together. Use the yarn tails to seam the cowl into a loop, matching up the colors. Weave in any remaining ends.

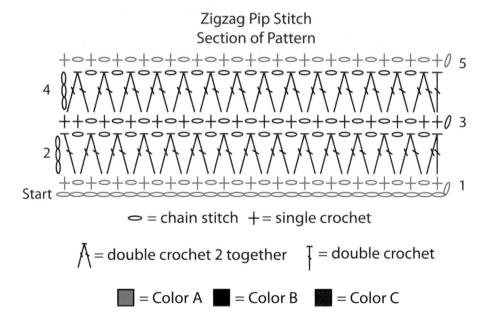

Zigzag Pip Stitch
Section of Pattern

$\circ$ = chain stitch $+$ = single crochet

$\wedge$ = double crochet 2 together $\top$ = double crochet

☐ = Color A ■ = Color B ■ = Color C

Techniques

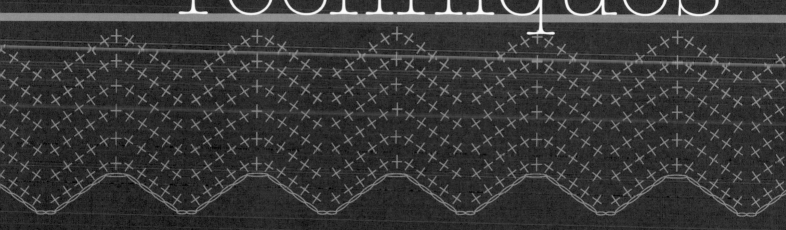

Traditional Crochet

In traditional crochet—the style most people are familiar with—only one stitch at a time is active. Each is worked to completion before the next stitch is begun. Stitch heights progress from the low-profile slip stitch through single crochet, half double crochet, double crochet, treble crochet, and beyond, based on how many times the yarn is wrapped around the hook and how the loops are pulled through other loops. Hooks for traditional crochet are usually 5 to 8 in. (13 to 20 cm) long and can be made of metal, plastic, bamboo, wood, or other materials.

CHAIN STITCH

1. Attach yarn to hook with slip knot. Yarn over, pull through.

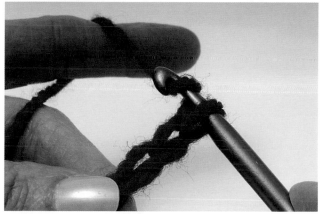

SLIP STITCH

1. Insert hook into work where instructed. (This stitch is often used to close a ring.)

2. Yarn over, pull through both loops.

SINGLE CROCHET

1. Insert hook into work where instructed. If you are working into the foundation chain, this will be the second chain from the hook.

2. Yarn over, pull up a loop.

3. Yarn over, pull through both loops.

HALF DOUBLE CROCHET

1. Yarn over.

2. Insert hook into work where instructed. If you are working into the foundation chain, this will be the third chain from the hook.

3. Yarn over, pull up a loop.

4. Yarn over, pull through all three loops.

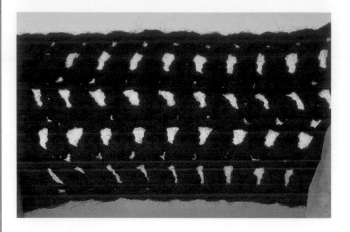

1. Yarn over.

2. Insert hook into the work where instructed. If you are working into the foundation chain, this will be the fourth chain from the hook.

3. Yarn over, pull up a loop.

4. Yarn over, pull through two loops.

5. Yarn over, pull through remaining two loops.

TREBLE CROCHET

3. Yarn over, pull up a loop.

1. Yarn over twice.

2. Insert hook into the work where instructed. If you are working into the foundation chain, this will be the fifth chain from the hook.

4. Yarn over, pull through two loops.

5. Yarn over, pull through two loops.

6. Yarn over, pull through remaining two loops.

CHANGE COLORS OR START A NEW YARN

1. Work in pattern as indicated. The photo shows double crochet fabric.

2. Work the next stitch until two loops remain on hook, no matter what type of stitch it is.

3. Drop the current yarn to the back. Yarn over with the new color and complete the stitch.

4. Continue to work with new yarn.

Tunisian Crochet

Tunisian crochet, also known as the "afghan stitch," combines aspects of crocheting and knitting. Like crocheting, it uses a hook and the same hand motions used in traditional crochet; as in knitting, loops are added to the hook so there are many active stitches at once. Tunisian crochet uses either a long hook with a stopper on the end or a shorter hook with a plastic extension to accommodate the many loops that will be on the hook at one time. Tunisian fabric can look knitted, woven, or textured and lacks the "loopy" appearance of traditional crochet.

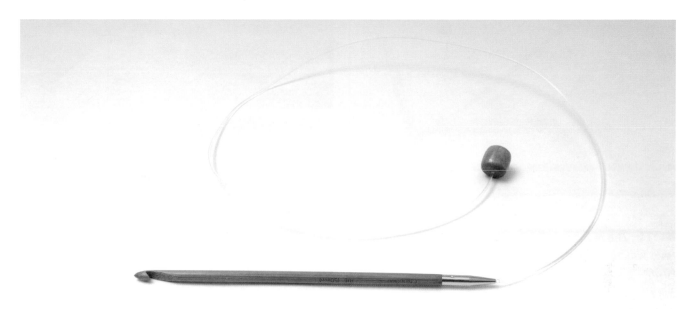

The photo shows a ChiaoGoo bamboo hook with a flexible extension and bead stopper.

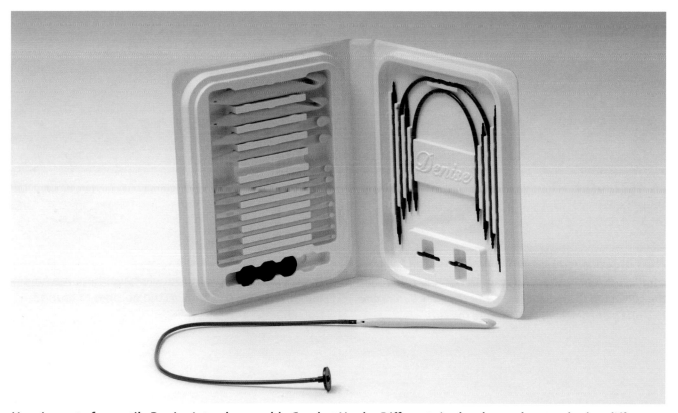

Here is a set of versatile Denise Interchangeable Crochet Hooks. Different size hooks can be attached to different lengths of plastic cord.

FOUNDATION ROW

Note: All Tunisian fabrics start with this basic row.

Foundation Row Forward

1. Make the number of chain stitches indicated in the pattern.

NOTE: *The number of Tunisian stitches on subsequent rows will be the same as the number of chains you start with.*

2. Insert hook in second chain from hook. Yarn over, pull up loop. There will be two loops on the hook.

NOTE: *To minimize the curl in Tunisian crochet, you could work into the back bump of the chain. I usually put the stitches in the regular place, not the back bump, and rely on steam blocking to eliminate the curl.*

3. Insert hook in the next chain. Yarn over, pull up loop. Each stitch adds another loop to the hook.

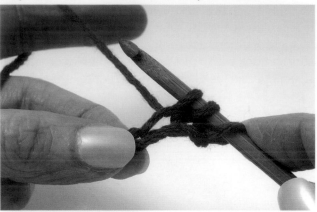

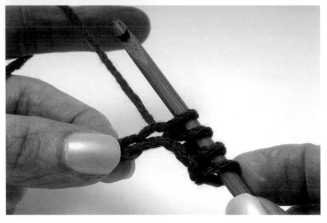

4. Continue in this fashion all the way across.

5. Count the loops. You should have the same number of loops on the hook as the number of foundation chains.

Foundation Row Return

1. Yarn over, pull through one loop.

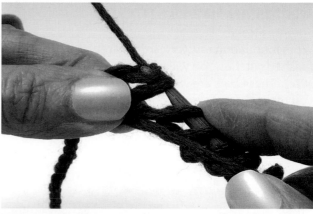

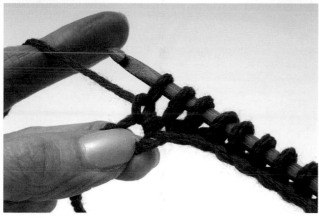

2. Yarn over, pull through two loops.

3. Repeat Step 2 all the way across until one loop remains on the hook.

NOTE: *This return method is referred to as the "standard return." Follow this procedure for the return pass unless instructed otherwise.*

TUNISIAN SIMPLE STITCH

Work foundation row forward and return. Look at the finished stitches. You will see a vertical bar for each stitch. These bars are what you will work behind as you make the Tunisian simple stitch forward pass.

1. Skip the first vertical bar that is on the far right side, directly below the hook.

2. Put the hook from right to left through the next vertical bar. Keep the hook to the front of the work. Yarn over, pull up a loop. There will be two loops on the hook.

3. Repeat Step 2 in each stitch across (except for the far left bar), adding a loop to the hook with each stitch.

4. To work the final stitch, identify the final vertical bar and the horizontal thread that runs behind it. Insert the hook so it is behind both of these threads. When viewed from the side, the two threads look like a backwards 6 for right-handers and a regular 6 for lefties.

Yarn over, pull up a loop. Count the loops. You should have the same number as you did on the foundation row.

5. Work standard return.

The photo below shows Tunisian simple stitch fabric.

TUNISIAN KNIT STITCH

Work foundation row forward and return. Look at the finished stitches. Each stitch has two "legs" in an upside-down V shape. Instead of keeping the hook to the front like you did in Tunisian simple stitch, for Tunisian knit stitch you will poke the hook from front to back through the center of each stitch.

Forward Pass
1. Skip the first vertical bar that is on the far right side, directly below the hook.

2. Put the hook from front to back through the next stitch. (Stretch the stitch out slightly to see where the two vertical legs are; go right between them, not between two stitches.) Yarn over. Pull up a loop. There will be two loops on the hook.

The photo below shows the hook poking out the back.

3. Repeat Step 2 in each stitch across (except for the far left bar), adding a loop to the hook with each stitch.

4. To work the final stitch, identify the final vertical bar and the horizontal thread that runs behind it. Insert the hook so it is behind both of these threads. When viewed from the side, the two threads look like a backwards 6 for right-handers and a regular 6 for lefties.

NOTE: *Even though you are working in Tunisian knit stitch, the final stitch is a Tunisian simple stitch. This creates stability along the left side.*

Yarn over, pull up a loop. Count the loops. You should have the same number as you did on the foundation row.

5. Work standard return.
The photo shows Tunisian knit stitch fabric.

Here is what it looks like on the back.

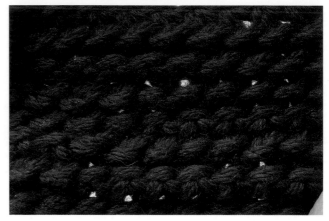

TUNISIAN PURL STITCH

Work foundation row forward and return. Look at the finished stitches. You will see a vertical bar for each stitch. These bars are what you will pick up as you work the Tunisian purl stitch forward pass. Keep the hook to the front of the work, as you did in Tunisian simple stitch.

Forward Pass

1. Skip the first vertical bar that is on the far right side, directly below the hook. Bring the yarn to the front of the hook.

2. Insert the hook into the next vertical bar, keeping the hook to the front of the work. The photo shows the yarn being held in place by my right index finger.

3. Let the yarn go. Bring it toward you in front of the stitch then back under the hook.

4. Yarn over, pull up a loop with that yarn. There will be two loops on the hook.

5. Repeat Step 1 in each stitch across (except for the far left bar), adding a loop to the hook with each stitch. Notice the "purl bump" in the front of each stitch.

6. To work the final stitch, identify the final vertical bar and the horizontal thread that runs behind it.

NOTE: *You will work a Tunisian simple stitch, not a Tunisian purl stitch, into the final stitch. Do not move the yarn to the front of the hook.*

Insert the hook so it is behind both of these threads. When viewed from the side, the two threads look like a backwards 6 for right-handers and a regular 6 for lefties.

Yarn over, pull up a loop. Count the loops. You should have the same number as you did on the foundation row.

7. Work standard return.

The photo shows Tunisian purl fabric.

Sometimes you will need to change colors for a stripe pattern. You will also need to start a new ball of yarn when the previous one runs out. The method is the same in both cases.

The ideal place to start a new yarn is at the end of a return pass.

1. Work return pass until two loops remain on hook. Drop first yarn to the back. Yarn over with new yarn.

Pull through both loops.

Pull old and new tails firmly to hold stitches in place.

2. Continue working with the new yarn, making sure you are using the working end of the yarn and not the short tail.

You can also change colors at the beginning of a return pass. Simply lay the new yarn over the hook, leaving a 3-inch (7.6 cm) tail, and begin the return pass with the new yarn.

FINAL ROW

The top row of Tunisian crochet looks looser than the previous rows because nothing is worked into it. One way to end the piece neatly is to work single crochet stitches across the top of that row.

1. Insert your hook as you would for whatever stitch pattern you're using. In the example, this is Tunisian simple stitch.

2. Yarn over, pull up loop, yarn over, pull through two loops. This creates a single crochet.

3. Repeat Step 2 across.

Helpful Hints for Tunisian Crochet

» Never turn your work. The right side is always facing you.

» Always skip the first vertical bar.

» Pull the yarn snug at the start of each row to keep the edge from getting baggy.

» The final stitch on every forward pass should be a Tunisian simple stitch, regardless of the other stitches on that row.

» Work the final stitch on the forward pass into the vertical bar and the horizontal bar behind it for stability. If you turn that edge toward you, those two threads should look like a backwards 6 for right-handers and a regular 6 for lefties.

» Make sure you count the last stitch of the forward pass and the first stitch of the return pass separately.

» You can work any stitch into any other type of stitch (for example, Tunisian purl stitch into Tunisian knit stitch, or Tunisian simple stitch into Tunisian purl stitch, and so on).

» Count! Check your stitch count regularly to make sure you did not miss picking up a stitch on a forward pass or mistakenly pull through the wrong number of loops on a return pass.

» To reduce the curl in Tunisian crochet, work the foundation row into the back bumps of the starting chains. Working a border around the piece helps, too. To eliminate any remaining curl, gently steam block your finished pieces.

Reading a Pattern

Before you begin working from a pattern, read through it thoroughly, paying particular attention to the information at the beginning, such as yarn, gauge, special stitches or stitch patterns, and notes. There is a wealth of information here that will aid you throughout the project. Note and practice any unfamiliar stitches, and crochet a gauge swatch using the stitches indicated in the gauge section. Adjust your hook size if necessary to meet gauge; this will put you on your way toward a successful garment in the size you intend. (Gauge is fairly flexible for the projects in this book, but it's best to get as close as possible.)

Make sure that you are familiar with the abbreviations used in the pattern. Most crochet patterns use standard abbreviations, but there may be some that are particular to a pattern; these will be noted. Read the master list in the back of this book (page 104) to familiarize yourself with the standard abbreviations, then refer to it as necessary when working the projects.

Patterns use parentheses ( ) or brackets [ ] to enclose a sequence of instructions meant to be repeated, either into a stitch or in a series of stitches. After the closing parenthesis or bracket, you'll be told how many times to repeat the instructions. For example, "[2 dc in next dc, 1 ch] twice" means to work 2 double crochet stitches in the next double crochet (from the row below), then 1 chain stitch, then 2 double crochet stitches in the next double crochet, then 1 chain stitch. Sometimes parentheses are just for explanatory information. For example, "(the center of three double crochet stitches in the corner)" clarifies the position of the stitch the pattern is referring to.

An asterisk * means to work the instructions following it as many more times as indicated. Sometimes the instructions will say, for example, "*2 dc in next st, sc in next st. Repeat from * to end of row." You would do the (2 double crochet, 1 single crochet) pattern until you got to the end of the row.

Reading a Symbol Chart

Crochet instructions can be given in text or charts. A visual representation of a pattern can be very useful in understanding how the item is made.

Here are some guidelines when reading charts:

First, look at the key to see which symbols represent which stitches. Make sure you know how to make the specified stitches.

When you are crocheting in rows for regular or Tunisian crochet, the pattern is charted row by row from the bottom up, starting with the foundation chain. Read the chart starting at bottom left for the chain.

For regular crochet, turn your work at the end of each row, following the chart. Read Row 1 right to left, Row 2 left to right, and so on.

In general, the only time you will actually work into a chain stitch is on Row 1, when you work into the foundation chain. On subsequent rows, if the symbol for the stitch you are supposed to make appears above one or more chains, work that stitch into the chain space rather than the chain stitch itself (unless the pattern or chart specifically says otherwise).

For Tunisian crochet, each row is worked in two passes: the forward pass (indicated by moving right to left in the chart) and the return pass (indicated by moving left to right in the chart). Patterns are charted in pairs of rows, starting after the foundation is complete. The bottom row in each pair represents the forward pass; the top row in each pair indicates the return pass. Read the bottom row right to left; read the top row left to right. Do not turn your work. The loop on the hook at the beginning of every forward pass, called the first vertical bar, counts as a stitch and is represented in charts by a Tunisian simple stitch symbol. Do not work an additional stitch in that spot.

When the final part of a Tunisian crochet project is worked in regular crochet stitches, treat that part of the chart as if it were for a regular crochet pattern.

When part of the pattern is repeated, that portion of the chart may be printed just once to save space.

Example of a traditional crochet chart.

Zigzag Pip Stitch
Section of Pattern

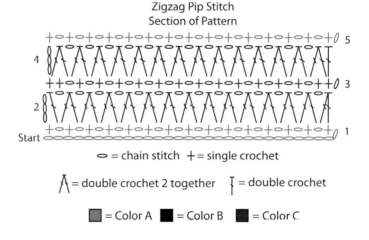

∘ = chain stitch   + = single crochet

⅄ = double crochet 2 together   ⊤ = double crochet

■ = Color A   ■ = Color B   ■ = Color C

Example of a Tunisian crochet chart.

Intarsia Arrows
Section of Pattern

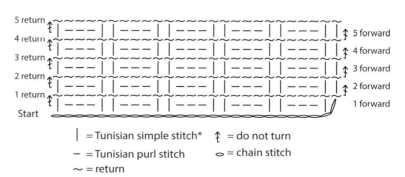

| = Tunisian simple stitch*   ↕ = do not turn

— = Tunisian purl stitch   ∘ = chain stitch

~ = return

When this symbol is the first stitch in the row, it represents the loop already on the hook.

Abbreviations

blo	back loop only
bch	beaded chain
bhdc	beaded half double crochet
ch(s)	chain(s)
dc	double crochet
dc2tog	double crochet 2 together
dtr/rf	double treble/raised front
hdc	half double crochet
LC	large cluster
lp(s)	loop(s)
lp st	loop st
quintr/rf	quintuple treble/raised front
rep	repeat
RS	right side
sc	single crochet
sk	skip
sl st	slip stitch
st(s)	stitch(es)
tr	treble crochet
Tfs	Tunisian full stitch
Tks	Tunisian knit stitch
Tps	Tunisian purl stitch
Tss	Tunisian simple stitch
Tss2tog	Tunisian simple stitch 2 together
WS	wrong side
yo	yarn over

CROCHET HOOK SIZES

Millimeter Range	U.S. Size Range*
2.25 mm	B-1
2.75 mm	C-2
3.25 mm	D-3
3.5 mm	E-4
3.75 mm	F-5
4 mm	G-6
4.5 mm	7
5 mm	H-8
5.5 mm	I-9
6 mm	J-10
6.5 mm	K-10½
8 mm	L-11
9 mm	M/N-13
10 mm	N/P-15
15 mm	P/Q
16 mm	Q
19 mm	S

* Letter or number may vary. Rely on the millimeter (mm) sizing.

SKILL LEVELS FOR CROCHET

1	◖□□□	**Beginner**	Projects for first-time crocheters using basic stitches. Minimal shaping.
2	◖■□□	**Easy**	Projects using yarn with basic stitches, repetitive stitch patterns, simple color changes, and simple shaping and finishing.
3	◖■■□	**Intermediate**	Projects using a variety of techniques, such as basic lace patterns or color patterns, mid-level shaping and finishing.
4	◖■■■	**Experienced**	Projects with intricate stitch patterns, techniques and dimension, such as non-repeating patterns, multicolor techniques, fine threads, small hooks, detailed shaping and refined finishing.

This Standards & Guidelines booklet and downloadable symbol artwork are available at: **YarnStandards.com**

Standard Yarn Weight System

Categories of yarn, gauge ranges, and recommended needle and hook sizes

Yarn Weight Symbol & Category Names	**0** LACE	**1** SUPER FINE	**2** FINE	**3** LIGHT	**4** MEDIUM	**5** BULKY	**6** SUPER BULKY	**7** JUMBO
Type of Yarns in Category	Fingering, 10-Count Crochet Thread	Sock, Fingering, Baby	Sport, Baby	DK, Light Worsted	Worsted, Afghan, Aran	Chunky, Craft, Rug	Bulky, Roving	Jumbo, Roving
Knit Gauge Range in Stockinette Stitch to 4 inches*	33–40 sts**	27–32 sts	23–26 sts	21–24 st	16–20 sts	12–15 sts	7–11 sts	6 sts and fewer
Recommended Needle in Metric Size Range	1.5–2.25 mm	2.25–3.25 mm	3.25–3.75 mm	3.75–4.5 mm	4.5–5.5 mm	5.5–8 mm	8–12.75 mm	12.75 mm and larger
Recommended Needle in U.S. Size Range	000 to 1	1 to 3	3 to 5	5 to 7	7 to 9	9 to 11	11 to 17	17 and larger
Crochet Gauge Ranges in Single Crochet to 4 inches*	32–42 double crochets**	21–32 sts	16–20 sts	12–17 sts	11–14 sts	8–11 sts	7–9 sts	6 sts and fewer
Recommended Hook in Metric Size Range	Steel*** 1.6–1.4 mm Regular hook 2.25 mm	2.25–3.5 mm	3.5–4.5 mm	4.5–5.5 mm	5.5–6.5 mm	6.5–9 mm	9–15 mm	15 mm and larger
Recommended Hook in U.S. Size Range	Steel 6, 7, 8*** Regular hook B–1	B–1 to E–4	E–4 to 7	7 to I–9	I–9 to K–10½	K–10½ to M–13	M–13 to Q	Q and larger

* GUIDELINES ONLY: The above reflect the most commonly used gauges and needle or hook sizes for specific yarn categories.
** Lace weight yarns are usually knitted or crocheted on larger needles and hooks to create lacy, openwork patterns. Accordingly, a gauge range is difficult to determine. Always follow the gauge stated in your pattern.
*** Steel crochet hooks are sized differently from regular hooks—the higher the number, the smaller the hook, which is the reverse of regular hook sizing.

Source: Craft Yarn Council of America's **www.YarnStandards.com**

BOOKS

Barnden, Betty. *The Crochet Stitch Bible*. Iola, WI: Krause Publications, 2004.

Guzman, Kim. *Tunisian Crochet Stitch Guide*. Little Rock, AR: Leisure Arts, Inc., 2013.

Matthews, Anne. *Vogue Dictionary of Crochet Stitches*. Newton, UK: David & Charles, 1987.

Reader's Digest. *The Ultimate Sourcebook of Knitting and Crochet Stitches*. Pleasantville, NY: Reader's Digest, 2003.

Silverman, Sharon Hernes. *Crochet Pillows*. Mechanicsburg, PA: Stackpole Books, 2011.

Silverman, Sharon Hernes. *Crochet Scarves*. Mechanicsburg, PA: Stackpole Books, 2012.

Silverman, Sharon Hernes. *Tunisian Crochet*. Mechanicsburg, PA: Stackpole Books, 2009.

Silverman, Sharon Hernes. *Tunisian Crochet for Baby*. Mechanicsburg, PA: Stackpole Books, 2014.

YARN

Bernat Yarns
www.yarnspirations.com

Blue Heron Yarns
www.blueheronyarns.com

Brown Sheep Company, Inc.
www.brownsheep.com

Crystal Palace Yarns
www.straw.com

Lion Brand Yarn Company
www.lionbrand.com

Madelinetosh Hand Dyed Yarns
www.madelinetosh.com

Plymouth Yarn Company, Inc.
www.plymouthyarn.com

Red Heart Yarn
www.redheart.com

Rowan
www.knitrowan.com

HOOKS

ChiaoGoo/Westing Bridge LLC
www.chiaogoo.com

Denise Interchangeable Knitting and Crochet
www.knitdenise.com

Stitch Diva Studios
www.stitchdiva.com

OTHER RESOURCES FOR CROCHETERS

Craft Yarn Council of America (CYCA)
The craft yarn industry's trade association has educational links and free projects.
www.craftyarncouncil.com

Crochet Guild of America (CGOA)
The national association for crocheters, CGOA sponsors conventions, offers correspondence courses, and maintains a membership directory.
www.crochet.org

Ravelry
This free online community for knitters, crocheters, and other fiber fans is *the* place to exchange information, manage projects, get advice on techniques, and keep up with everything yarn-related.
www.ravelry.com

Acknowledgments

Thanks to everyone who helped this book become a reality.
I am grateful to those who provided supplies: Demian Savits and
Barbara Lundy Stone of Blue Heron Yarns; Peggy Jo Wells of Brown
Sheep Company, Inc.; Susan C. Druding, Cathy Campbell, and Andrea Gaeta
of Crystal Palace Yarns; Brandyce Pechillo of Lion Brand Yarn Company;
Vanessa Ewing of Plymouth Yarn Company, Inc.; and Emily Berney of Spin-
rite LP.

Many thanks to Mark Allison, Editor; Candice Derr, Assistant Editor;
and Judith M. Schnell, Publisher of Stackpole Books. Also thank you to
cover and page layout designer Tessa Sweigert and chart designer Lindsey
Stephens.

Top-quality photography is essential for a crochet book. Deep gratitude
to the photographers whose work appears in this book: Daniel Shanken
(model photography) and Alan Wycheck (technique photography). And to
our models who made the cowl designs come alive.

Thanks to the Craft Yarn Council of America for permission to reprint
standards, to the Crochet Guild of America (CGOA) for industry information
and news, and to The National NeedleArts Association (TNNA) for its support of yarn industry professionals.

The debt that can never be repaid adequately is to my friends and fam-
ily for their love and support. Special thanks to my mother, Babe Hernes;
my sister, Helene Silverman; my husband, Alan; and our sons, Jason and
Steven.

Visual Index

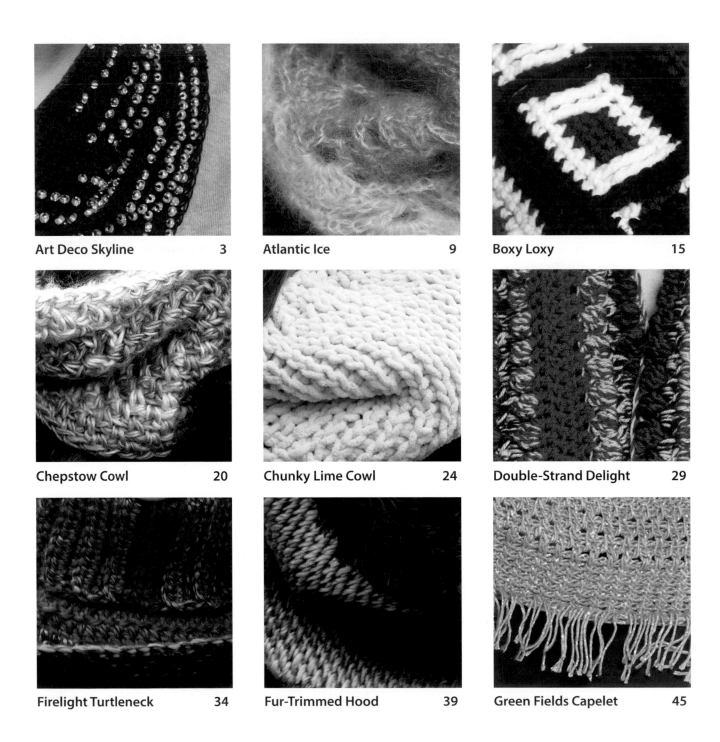

Leading the Way in Crafts

Discover inspiration and tips for your next project!